Around the World in Search for the Right Shoe

An Immigrant's Experiences Between Two Different Cultures

by

Irina Martkovich

DORRANCE
PUBLISHING CO
EST. 1920
PITTSBURGH, PENNSYLVANIA 15238

The contents of this work, including, but not limited to, the accuracy of events, people, and places depicted; opinions expressed; permission to use previously published materials included; and any advice given or actions advocated are solely the responsibility of the author, who assumes all liability for said work and indemnifies the publisher against any claims stemming from publication of the work.

All Rights Reserved
Copyright © 2023 by Irina Martkovich

No part of this book may be reproduced or transmitted, downloaded, distributed, reverse engineered, or stored in or introduced into any information storage and retrieval system, in any form or by any means, including photocopying and recording, whether electronic or mechanical, now known or hereinafter invented without permission in writing from the publisher.

Dorrance Publishing Co
585 Alpha Drive
Pittsburgh, PA 15238
Visit our website at *www.dorrancebookstore.com*

ISBN: 979-8-8852-7357-2
eISBN: 979-8-8852-7482-1

INTRODUCTION

This is a memoir about how I emigrated from Soviet Latvia to America in 1979. It's about the pain of leaving my country, my family, my friends, my books, my cat. Knowing that I would never see them again, never touch them, never contact them, never send them a letter, never see their photograph.

Why, why are you leaving, my friends were asking. I managed to joke. Well, I answered, being such a tall person I can't find proper footwear in this country. The largest size for women that Soviet factories produced was size 11, I wear size 12. Now try wearing shoes a size smaller than yours for an hour, then imagine wearing them for a lifetime.

After emigrating to the US the first thing I did was buy a pair of comfortable shoes and then I started writing extensively about America. That's how the book "Around The World In Search Of The Right Shoe" came into being.

Then things started to change.

AROUND THE WORLD IN SEARCH FOR THE RIGHT SHOE

I was born in the cold month of February in the city of Riga, Latvia and named after my maternal aunt Irina. I hope that naming me presented my parents with less of a problem than naming my sister who came into this world seven years later. My father wanted her to be named Kristya, which I believe is a Swedish name. To the Slavic ear this name sounded too harsh, so my mother was dead against it. Whatever name was suggested by my mother was vehemently rejected by my father. Finally my mother got so annoyed that she told him to go to the Office of Birth Registration and choose whatever name he desired. My dad stormed out of the house. At the Office of Birth Registration he asked a big Slavic woman who was guarding an oak desk for the book of girls' names. Out of a drawer she produced a heavy brown volume. He opened it at random and pointed out a name on the page without even looking at it. The woman dutifully filled out the forms. When my mother asked him what name he had chosen for their newborn, he said he didn't know and told her to look in the papers. She opened the envelope and saw that their daughter had been named Natalie, the name both of them equally disliked.

Years later my sister Natalie and I ended up living in two different parts of the world far away from Latvia. Not long ago I learned that had we chosen to remain in Latvia, we wouldn't be considered citizens of our country of birth because our parents were not Latvian born. Latvia adopted this law after the Soviet rule. My father, born in Odessa, and my mother, born in the Urals, ended up in Latvia after WWII, following my grandfather who had been assigned as a head physician of a ward in a big military hospital in Riga. My grandfather was a well-known heart specialist who got his education in Germany and France and spoke six languages. He came from a poor family. The woman he married was rich. Her early death from a heart disease left a deep scar of sorrow both on him and his son. My grandfather never remarried and neither of the men ever spoke her name. I guess my grandfather felt that being a heart specialist, he had failed as a physician and my dad felt abandoned. They hardly ever spoke to each other; they would meet at the table, eat in silence and part when the meal was over. When they did speak they fought bitterly. The bone of contention was the Soviet regime. My grandfather believed that it was progressive and made many people's lives better. My dad hated it passionately with that final everlasting hatred.

They had no meeting ground. One day I was actually surprised to find out that my grandfather was my father's father. I was a very young child but to this day I clearly remember the shock of this discovery. I was surprised because I witnessed the silence that was set up between them; theirs didn't feel like a father and son relationship.

The little that I know about my grandmother, I have learned from her sister Sonya who was also a physician. I know that her name was Taba, that she laughed a lot and was quite mischievous. She studied medicine and became a doctor. After giving birth to my father, Tabochka, as her sister lovingly called her, developed a heart condition, from which she subsequently died. As I look at her picture I see a beautiful woman in a long dress looking straight at me, her face dire, and serious. The photo was taken at the time when women had not yet learned to flirt with a camera. There are thick bushes behind her, and it always seemed to me that I could see the face of her early death lurking in the background, looking at me through the shadows of the foliage.

As my father was growing up, he developed a rare gift as an artist. So powerful was his gift that years later his former co-student who became an editor in a big publishing company found my father and asked him to illustrate a collection of works by the writer Alexander Green. Though flattered by this offer, my father declined it saying that he no longer painted. His demanding job of a chief mechanic on a ship left him no time for artistic pursuits.

My father and I shared tremendous love for the sea. It was coded in my genes from my father's. In fact, he risked his life to become a marine. When WWII started and he was drafted into the Red Army, he learned that young men were separated into soldiers and marines depending on a certain number in their papers. He forged the number, and thus became a marine instead of a soldier. In the Soviet Union this was a crime punishable by imprisonment, but he was never caught. Years later his first wife who was privy to this fact, persistently blackmailed him and my grandfather regularly sent her money to buy her silence and save his only son from jail. After WWII my father became a sea engineer.

I was such a fat baby that cotton pads had to be placed in the folds of my legs to prevent skin irritation. I was growing so fast that nobody could believe my age. Once my mother took me to the Zoo. The entrance to the Zoo was free for children under seven. I was six and a half. "How old is your child?" a zoo attendant demanded suspiciously as we approached the gate. "Six and a half," answered my mother sheepishly. "What? Are you telling me that this child is six and a half years old?" The Zoo attendant raised her voice appealing to the visitors standing on line. There was a whisper of disbelief and people looked at my mother with disapproval. Without another word my mother went to the box office and purchased me a ticket. I remember this incident clearly for I was aware of my mother's embarrassment and understood that I was the cause of it. This was the first time I realized that there was something wrong with me. After the incident I continued growing for another ten years. People who met me for the first time invariably asked me if I was taller than my parents to which I always replied," Yes, I am taller than my mother, my father and even our wardrobe." In the end I grew to be slightly over six feet tall, which is tall even for a Latvian. Although Latvia is a very small country, it gives birth to very tall people. It has been observed that when identical twins served in the Soviet army, the one who served in Latvia would grow to be five centimeters taller than his twin who was stationed elsewhere in the Soviet Union.

I never felt self-conscious about my height though because my father was partial to tall people. In fact, he fell in love with my mother because of her height. Once my uncle told me how my father announced to him so proudly that he had met this incredibly tall woman who wore size forty-one shoes. It was my mother. Clearly the marriage where the big shoe size was the main attraction was not happily destined, but they did get married, produced two off spring and stayed together for almost half a century until death parted them.

Before my mother got married, she used to work as a bookkeeper. Once she got married, she stopped working. In her late years she tried to resume working but by then she was plagued by so many health problems that she was no longer able to hold a job. One of her problems was high blood pressure. The medication she received for it made her depressed. Sadly, this is how I remember my mom: always irritated, angry, depressed and sick. During her late years, she developed a problem with her feet and had difficulty finding proper footwear. Once she brought home a pair of shoes purchased at a second hand store. The shoes were quite ugly but fit her like a pair of gloves. When I touched their soft maroon top the expensive leather seemed to melt under my fingers the way good chocolate melted on my tongue. My father looked at the shoes and said. "This footwear must have been produced in America. Nobody else would make or wear such ugly shoes." He was right, for the label said 'Made in America.' That's probably when my dream was born to go to the country where all people wore comfortable footwear.

In fact, when my friends asked me why I decided to emigrate, I told them half jokingly that it was because I couldn't find the shoes my size. 41 was the largest size the Soviet factories used to produce, and I wore size 42. Now try wearing the shoes one size smaller than yours for an hour, save throughout your childhood and adolescence.

Finding the right clothes also presented a problem. Everything was either too short or too small for me. I would hear my girlfriends discuss what they would wear at the upcoming party.

- I've got myself a silk dress, one of them would say.
- I will wear a new velvet skirt, the other one would announce happily. Then they would turn to me.
- How about you, Irina?
- I will wear a new bag, I would respond gloomily, "for this is the only thing my size that I could find in the stores.

Once I had even been excluded from the May Day parade, the act of solidarity with the world proletariat, participation in which was obligatory for every high school student and teacher. All students were required to wear blue velvet berets that were distributed to us by our class supervisor. Well, not only was I a Big Foot, I was obviously a Big Head too, for none of the berets fit me. Having tried about a dozen of them, I was dismissed from the demonstration. "Go home, Irina," said our class supervisor, "I cannot have your uncovered head sticking out on May Day Parade." And off I went.

Unfortunately my upbringing contributed to the problem. My grandfather was an ardent lover of classical music. Because of his poor eyesight, one of us children had to accompany him on his frequent trips to the concerts at the philharmonic. Since I was the oldest of his two grandchildren, this responsibility often fell on my shoulders. Years later I was surprised to hear classical music playing in the greenhouses of the Himalayan Institute in the Poconos. "It's so that the plants would grow better," the worker there told me. That explains why my sister Natalie grew up to be five centimeters shorter than I did. She has been exposed to less classical music than I was.

My father who passionately hated the Soviet regime started preparing us for leaving the Soviet Union a quarter of century in advance. I began learning the English language from a private teacher when I was only five years old, my sister Natalie, when she was seven. Yet, my father wanted us to see the reality clearly. "Remember," he used to say, "everything bad that they are telling about us and we are telling about them is true." In the end both of his daughters have emigrated. I went to live in America. After my parents' death Natalie and her daughter Anna Maria immigrated to Israel.

When I was sixteen and decided to study languages. My family was dead set against it. My grandfather was more outspoken than anybody else. "Studying languages is not a profession," he said to me firmly,"It is a hobby." And who would know better than him. My grandfather, Dr. Mordkovich knew Russian,English, French, German, Yiddish and Latin. He read medical journals in French and English. When I needed help with my Latin I ran to him. What could I say? They were right. In those times finding a job for an English teacher in Latvia was not an easy task. Many of them had to abandon their professions and work in offices. Yet against my family's wishes and against all common sense I set out to enter the Faculty of Foreign Languages at the Latvian State University. Looking back I have to say that the profession of an English teacher has brought me little wealth, yet it has fed me pretty steadily throughout my life. In Latvia I used to work as an English teacher at the University, give private lessons at home and earn a pretty good income from that. When I set out to immigrate to America my father again pleaded with me. "Where are you going?" He said. "Every dog knows English in America. You have no profession to survive in that country." Yet against all odds and ends my profession has fed me even in America. Shortly after my arrival I began teaching English as a Second Language at the City University of New York where I taught for over eighteen years. When my husband and I moved out of the city to the suburbs of Long Island I got a job at a local community college where I am presently teaching ESL. All my life I have instinctively followed the formula that in my later years I heard from Swami Rama of the Himalayas. "Think the way you feel and act the way you think. Everything else will result in neurosis." There is another formula that I try to adhere to which belongs to Swami Bua an ancient Yogi who used to teach yoga in New York till his death at the age of 115. "If the body does the right thing," he used to say, "the mind will find the answer." These two formulas are a recipe for a healthy and satisfying life.

A SECOND LIFE

Today is the day. Two days ago, I received a postcard informing me that on June 19, 1979 at 9:30 am, I am expected to be at the Office of Emigration. I approach a six story redbrick building. With the lush green ivy climbing its walls it's no different from any other building on the spacious Gorki Street, yet everybody knows that those who are headed there intend to emigrate from Latvia. Passersby view me with curiosity. I try to pretend I'm just one of them, that I have nothing to do with this somber looking building, and I wish to God it were true. I wish I had never started it; I wish I had been born in another country, on another planet, and in another solar system. I wish all this were happening to someone else, and that I was watching a movie. I can no longer pretend that I am passing this building on my way to work. I open the door.

I hear a low hum of voices coming from upstairs. On the second floor, the staircase is full of people. I wonder why there are so many people. It is my fight. I don't want any crowds. I've never felt like a part of a crowd. I've always avoided it. Here for the first time in my life, I become part of one. No one talks. Only family members whisper among themselves. From time to time, the doors swing open, spitting out a stern-faced brunette in a green military uniform that is too narrow for her heavy hips.

I was born too late to know what World War II was like, and I hope and pray I am born too soon for the Third one. But here I understand for the first time in my life what real fear is; the fear I've seen in movies and read about in books. Now it's happening to me. I see tears in a man's eyes. I've never seen a man cry before. Panic seizes me, but it's too late to run

7

away. I've done something that will live with my family and me for the rest of our lives. If I don't get permission to emigrate, I'll rot for years at some degrading job which, rather than killing me will make me a living lesson for posterity. Never will I be able to teach again. I will be morally unfit to do so. My dad will lose his job whether I emigrate or not, just because I have applied for permission to leave the country; and Natalie will always carry a stigma of having a morally unfit sister.

God, I'll never ask you for anything else. Just help me this one time, please, help me to get out of here.

The staircase leads to an anteroom which is too small to hold all the people who have come. The brunette in a green military uniform barks,"Sit down! Why are you all standing? It's impossible to pass through!" It is obvious that there are not enough chairs for even half of the people who are here today. Besides, fear refuses to sit down; it can only walk or stand.

I return to the staircase. There is nowhere to hide my face. People are everywhere, and they avoid looking at one another. The wait goes for forty, fifty minutes, maybe more. By now I have lost track of time. Meanwhile, friends and relatives arrive. Small whirlpools of conversation start and die. In the middle of it all, I hear my name; somebody has called my name from the anteroom. The voice keeps calling out names. I enter the room together with a few others. The rest are ordered to leave. In a lifeless tone, as if someone else were moving her lips, the woman says we've been granted permission to leave Soviet Latvia; that we must leave within two months, or else pay heavy penalties.

I am listening, but I don't hear. Rather, I hear, but I don't understand. Oh, are they really letting me go?

We are told to write what documents are necessary for us to get our visas. I start frantically fumbling through my pockets. Pen and paper. How strange these words sound to me. Oh, here is a pen, but I have no paper. Someone next to me hands me a sheet. She is already in the middle of the ninth sentence. What did she say? What is she saying? My hand refuses to write. I am split. A part of me is listening, another is writing, and these two selves refuse to cooperate. I'm disconnected, but I see some signs appear on the white sheet before me. I am all right. I'm making notes. And then it comes. An awful pain sweeps over me.

The woman, the room, and the people are soaked in pain! Pain! Congratulations, you've won the major battle of your life.

I walk out of the building. I make sure my face shows no emotion. There is emptiness in my stomach. Up to this moment, I knew everything that was going to happen to me. I also knew what would happen if I got a refusal. I didn't allow myself to think of a happy ending. It was kind of a suicidal act for me. I thought I would die, and I was ready for it. But I was left to live. From now on, I cannot know my future. I am separated from those who could tell me about what happens on the other side by the borders of my country. It's as if the path I've been on is suddenly lost in the grass. It just stops.

Slowly I'm coming to life. I notice green leaves, sun, birds, and children in the park. I am very tired, but it is good to be alive, and the great noise of life fills my ears as if someone has turned on the sound for me.

I meet someone on the street, someone who doesn't know anything about what has just happened to me. We talk about my work, (which I no longer have), and my upcoming vacation (which is never to be), and my friends, (whom I'll never see again), and I savor the taste of life on my lips. I have been granted a second life. From now on, everything that is going to happen to me will be as new as life is to a newborn. I will be helpless and dumb. The only difference is that there will be no mother beside me. There will be nobody. Now I am on my own.

The next day I go to Old Riga to say farewell to the city where I was born thirty years ago. Walking towards the Daugava River I turn the corner of an old cobble stone street. It is early evening. In the light of the dying sun the two century old buildings and courtyards assume a mysterious, almost eerie appearance of theatrical props. The spire of the old cathedral pierces the marble sky and the beauty of Old Riga penetrates my heart with a bitter powerful force. I am getting close to the Daugava River; the breeze smells of water. As I am turning yet another corner I bump into my friend Peteris. For a while we walk side by side and I am glad I don't have to look him in the eye. He feels something is wrong and like a devoted pet tries to look into my soul. Yet my soul is silent. It has already been frozen, packed and waiting to be transported to Vienna where it would finally defrost in a three day crying spree. As the violet dusk finally descends onto the world, we hug and part forever.

That night I call all the people I love and trust, and invite them over to say our good-byes. I invite only the closest, most trusted friends, for the rest of the world should never learn that I am leaving, my dad warns me. I laugh; the Communist Party is like Kirillian photography. They know what you are going to do even before you yourself know it. But my father is right. My friends, worthy of my trust never let out a word. My dad, having signed his consent for my emigration at the office of his residence rather than at work, like everybody else does, will be able to continue working in the Baltic fleet for another decade.

My friends arrive one by one. We drink Caberne, and talk about books, courage, and other important things. We argue and joke and smile at each other, in celebration. In the middle of our conversation, someone turns to me and says,"You will write to us, won't you, Irina?" "Sure, I will," I answer. We are silent for a while, and then our conversation resumes. I walk back and forth with cups, plates, and wine, and no one seems to be paying any special attention to me. You see, we avoid looking at each other, because we know that we will never see each other again. Never! I have a curious feeling of not being with them any more, of being already somewhere else, and just watching them from afar, all those dear, precious people. I watch them the way a soul watches its body at a funeral.

Here is my friend Olga... a lovely, tiny, nymph-like creature, always smiling, always excited about one thing or another, always ready to celebrate life, even if it is on account of my departure into the land of no return. A couple of years later, she'll be able to emigrate, too. Her husband, a six foot four inch former marine, five years her junior, will die from a heart attack in Brazil.

Katya is hiding behind her big golden-rimmed glasses, and a cup of tea. She will die in three years, but nobody knows of the cancer that is eating at her insides, yet.

Tamara, my English teacher is presiding over the table. Calm and collected, she looks like a high priestess. A survivor of a concentration camp, she is glad that I got a chance to escape. Five years later, she'll be paralyzed by a stroke. She'll die alone in her apartment, unable to call for help.

Alyosha, a talented physicist, will end up working as a night guard to support his wife and two children. His Ph. D. in Physics will only be a detriment to his survival.

Life will be kind to our dear Adolf, our physician. He will marry a nurse. It will be a happy marriage. The union will produce three round-headed, dark-eyed boys.

I will meet Misha again ten years later in London, where he will be working for BBC. Eventually, he'll end up back in Russia, working for the Israeli Embassy.

Datse, who is engaged to an African student of the Moscow University, is about to get married, and leave the country with her husband. This will never come to pass. The KGB will set up surveillance over her, listen to her phone conversations, and change the contents of her fiancé's telegrams. When all of the above fails to dissuade her from marrying a foreigner, she'll receive an invitation for a routine check-up at a clinic, which will reveal the presence of tuberculosis. She will be placed in the hospital and undergo a mandatory treatment. After a year, they will tell her that they have made a mistake in diagnosis, and that she doesn't have tuberculosis. She'll then be allowed to leave the hospital, her health having been ruined by heavy doses of toxic medication.

But it will be Tolik, our beloved Tolik, the gentle giant, the heart of our parties, who will meet the most tragic end of all. He will develop a persecution mania. Delirious, he'll jump out of the window of his five-story apartment, holding his three year-old daughter firmly in his arms. She will die instantly. Two months later, having learned of what he has done, he will throw himself on the railroad tracks and be crushed by the train.

Anita, a brilliant college professor, will eventually get her PhD. Many years later, I'll be showing her around New York, which she will visit with the Latvian business delegation in the capacity of a translator. Among other places I will take her to Balducci's which happens to be an expensive food store in the middle of Greenwich Village. Balducci has an impressive display of all kinds of food. It is in the fruit and vegetable section, at the sight of six different types of mushrooms that she'll burst into tears. "Americans will never understand us," she'll say to me.

When I see my little sister next, she'll be fifteen years older. Then I'll also meet my niece, Annushka, for the first time. Funny, brown-eyed, and redheaded, she'll be eight years of age.

I look at my friends. They are young, healthy and vibrant, and I try to imprint their faces in my memory, so that I could take their images with me. At midnight, we hug and part. We are strong, and we do not cry. That night, I sleep without dreams.

The next morning, a taxi driver sees the size of my suitcase, and asks if I am going to Moscow. I answer, yes. We come to a railway station where my friends are waiting for me. All of a sudden, heavy rain pours down, and we rush under the roof of the railway station, struggling to find each other in a crowd that is pushing upon us from all sides. We long to touch each other for the last time, and say all those important words we've saved for the last moment. But the moment never comes, for although the rain stops, the train arrives, and I must climb in right away. It's an enormous crowd, twice as many tickets sold as there should have been. People fight for seats. Once inside, I can't get to a window, because of the constant chain of people passing in front of me. My friends wait on the platform for a long time, hoping that they'll be able to catch the last glimpse of me, and as the train moves, they walk with it. But, I never see them. A very drunk man, tall, thin, worn-out, his breath reeking of vodka leans over me, demanding that I should give my seat to his relative who has a ticket for the same seat.

BREST BOUND

The year is 1979. On the train the Polish citizens returning home from their trip to the Soviet Union are cursing loudly. There is a mess in Poland too, they say, but they have never seen anything like this. Twice as many tickets sold as there are seats on the train! The Jews are silent; some in shock, others in tears. Having found themselves between the cursing and the crying, everyday Russian travelers look bewildered. They never seem to comprehend why so many people on the train are in tears.

We learn that at a certain juncture of our journey the train will split into two parts. The first part will remain at a station, while the second part will proceed to Brest, a town on the border with Poland. I'm traveling in the first part of the train, so is my former student Fima, his wife Galina, their five-year-old daughter Dina and his mother-in-law Sofi. Since there won't be enough time to transfer our luggage when the split occurs, it has to be done now. We team up and carry our suitcases to the back of the train. Being unable to go through the cars, filled to the brim with people, we go down the steps at each station and drag the heavy suitcases along the platform until the train is ready to leave. When the conductor blows his whistle, we climb up the steps and wait till the next stop. When we finally arrive in Brest they demand that we pay again for the already pre-paid tickets to Vienna. They know that we are not going to complain about it. Who is going to complain to whom? We are about to leave the country, and we are not coming back. We pay again for the prepaid tickets.

BREST

At customs in Brest, my old high-heeled winter boots have attracted a sergeant's attention. He is repeatedly poking a screwdriver into their patched-up heels searching for something and simultaneously observing my reaction. "What is he looking for?" I ask the man standing next to me. "Diamonds," he responds. I can't help smiling. "What's your profession? "The sergeant hollers at me. Teacher, I say. Teachers don't own diamonds. He lets me pass. I follow a young couple that has just cleared the customs and we cross the gate, the point of no return. The young woman before me turns around to her mother, brother and two sisters who are standing on the other side of the gate. She is trembling, a scared animal. The woman and her family are looking at each other with such sorrow that my heart cringes.

Two hours later, the sorrowful young woman and her husband, Fima,my former student his family and I are all boarding the train. It's noon. The sun is high in the sky. The wind is picking up. For the last time I breathe in the air of my motherland. Farewell. Farewell. Farewell. I will never, never see you again.

AUSTRIA

In Vienna, we are placed in a fifth floor apartment. There is a brothel right above us on the sixth floor. In the evening we hear music and the soft laughter of women in elegant gowns socializing with their clientele on the balcony upstairs. The young women are very attractive and come in all races, shapes and colors; the evening breeze brings the smell of their French perfume into our roach-ridden apartment. Here roaches are everywhere: on the table, in the sink and on the stove. Not everyone takes to roaches well. We hear about an emigre who has returned to the Office of Housing to express his dismay over his living conditions. There he was offered a catalogue of the best hotels in Vienna and asked to choose the one to his liking after which they put him and his suitcases in a cab and sent him to his destination. He came back in an hour. They asked him if he had found the accommodations in the hotel to his liking. "I did," the man said seething with anger, "but I've got no money to pay for it." "If you have no money, sir, you'll have to go back to your apartment."

I share the *roach-ridden* apartment with Fima, his tall thin long-legged wife Galina, their five-year-old daughter Dina and a father and son from Lithuania, Nikolai and Lev, both doctors. Fima's mother-in-law, Sofi, has since departed to join her elder daughter in Israel. The father-doctor, a man in his late fifties with a white long beard reminds me of Karl Marx. In his deep voice he repeatedly lectures us on the danger that roaches pose to our health and instructs us to sterilize our dishes and silverware in boiling water. We do as he says. Doctor Nikolai stays in the apartment to guard his numerous leather suitcases. The rest of us with nothing to guard go out to see the city. Vienna with its old red brick buildings, cobble stone streets and bright lush greenery is an illustration to an old fairy tale. We marvel at the bright flowerbeds, neatly manicured lawns and stores filled with all kinds of food and clothes. In one of them Fima's five-year-old daughter Dina has a fit. She bawls, cries and stomps her little feet. She wants everything she sees. Now! The parents drag the screaming child out. of the store. We travel to the Vienna market where the sight of so many coveted fruit and vegetables makes my heart jump. Having come out of Soviet Latvia we know little more than the taste of oranges, lemons, tangerines and an occasional grapefruit. We learn the names of many colorful fruits that are laid out on the tables. I am amused by the small brown firm and furry kiwi, the yellow freckled sweet smelling bananas, the clumsy enormity of a succulent ugly fruit, and the rough brownness of a Chinese pear. We bathe in the sweet smell of honeydew melons and get drunk on all those shapes, smells and colors. Having bought one of each of the colorful fruit we go home to taste them for the first time.

The next day we take a tram to an Immigration Office where we are instructed to fill out endless forms. As I am writing down the names of my parents, my sister and my relatives,.the names evoke their faces, and tears start rolling down my cheeks. There is no stopping them , This is the first time I have gotten to cry since the whole saga of immigration started two and a half years ago and I cry for three straight days. On the morning of the fourth day everybody has had enough of looking at my red swollen face. Galina suggests that we should go see a movie. The movie theater is right across the street. We go in and pay for the tickets. The movie has already started. We cautiously make our way in the dark and sit down. Well, it's a distraction all right for it happens to be a porno movie filled with sex, violence and motorcycles. This is the first porno movie we have seen in our life. No such movies are shown in the Soviet movie theaters. When it is over and the lights go on, we find that we are the only two women in the all-male audience. Quickly we exit the theater, run across the road and burst into an uncontrollable fit of laughter. The elevator is broken and we climb up the stairs spilling our laughter all over the steps. On the way up we meet a contraband dealer. He is here to purchase some cotton sheets. "Young ladies," he appeals to us, "I've been in this business for years, but I swear I've never seen an immigrant laugh so hard. Come to think of it, it's been a long time since I saw anybody laugh so hard. Would you please,

please, tell me what's so funny." We moan, wave him aside and continue on our way to the fifth floor, laughing all the way to the top.

Two days later we board the train to Italy.

ITALY

Loud women's voices from the yard awaken me early in the morning. I don't know Italian and therefore do not understand why they are so agitated.

It sounds like they are being assaulted. I run to the window in my pink nightgown and look out into the yard. A big-busted Italian woman in a long skirt holding a bag full of vegetables is demonstrating them to her girlfriend on the third floor and that's what all the shouting is about. Relieved I return to bed but am unable to go back to sleep. It is way too hot. It is late August and the temperature in Rome must be over a 100 degrees Fahrenheit.

In the evening we are served huge plates filled with spaghetti drowning in tomato sauce. After the meal an old lady thoroughly scrubs the wooden tables. A man who is sitting at our table tells us that the old lady arrived in Rome with her daughter and her daughter's family. One morning she woke up and found that her family has departed having abandoned her in Rome. Now she earns her living by helping them in the kitchen.

In the Soviet Union we were warned about unemployment, crime and poverty but no one ever warned us about heat. Having come from Latvia with a temperate climate, I find this heat to be unbearable. I fully understand what a fish feels when it is dragged out of the water. Last night we experienced our first Italian thunderstorm. It was so hot and the thunder was so loud that it sounded like the earth itself split in half. In the morning I can take a full breath of fresh air for the first time since arriving in Italy. Next day while we are traveling in search for an apartment away from this scorching hell, I keep thinking about Haitian students' reaction to a Moscow winter that I had observed years ago while traveling in Russia. I was supposed to collect materials for a series of lectures on English children's literature for the course that I was supposed to teach in the upcoming semester. Every morning I would take a Metro to the center of Moscow and from there change for the bus. "Excuse me could you tell me how to get to the Foreign Language Library?" "Sure" I said to the tall dark thin Haitian man. "You're in luck I'm headed there." "Thank you," he said. "Where are you from," I asked. "Haiti." The bus stopped and the man and the group of Haitian students got out. As we are walking briskly down the street I hear a very strange sound behind me. I turn around and see that more than half of them are crying and moaning loudly in agony.

As I am reliving that moment I see that my train stops in a small seaside resort town called Ladispoli where I am to share an apartment with three other families. In Ladispoli a cool sea breeze relieves the summer heat. It's a lovely little town. From the back of the buildings the waves of bright blue flowers climb over the roof and from there descend onto the balconies. The houses look like ships drowning in the ocean of flowers.

At an interview in the Immigration Office I gladly accept the job as a medical interpreter. In the morning I work for two very likable Italian doctors translating their patients' complaints from Russian into English. In the afternoon I go to the beach and watch Italian women and children laugh and play in the waves of the warm emerald waters of the Adriatic Sea. Their happy carefree suntanned faces are in sharp contrast to the somber pasty faces of my compatriots, who even though they have already lost their first twenty pounds and are stuffed in their western jeans with their heavy thighs, they remain sad and forlorn. Yesterday I was watching a three-year-old black baby crawling among sunbathers and biting their toes. There was a lot of screaming and laughing.

In the evening I swim with the guys far away from the shore and play ball in the water. As we swim back, we see a crowd of Italians who are waiting for us to get out of the water. They just stand there watching us. I am alarmed. The next day I ask the Italian doctor who I am working for if there are any dangerous sea animals or underwater currents in the sea. "I have not seen any locals swim far away from the shore," I say. "Don't worry, Irina, there is no danger in these waters," he says calmly. "Then why do people stare at us like this when we come out of the water?" I ask. "Well," he says, "It is simple. Italians are lazy. They would never swim so far away from the shore, and are curious to see who does."

There is plenty of work. In Italy all subconscious fears of America imbedded for decades in the Russian mind by Soviet propaganda surface and the immigrants pour into the doctor's office with all kinds of complaints. They desperately want to delay their departure to America. What if after all the horrors described by Soviet propaganda about the US are true? The fear of America raging in the soul of a Soviet immigrant is akin to that in the soul of a tribe member who has broken a taboo. In primitive societies people die from such fear. The bodies and minds of Russian immigrants have gone into shock. A quiet shy lady of about forty hasn't had a bowel movement in over two weeks. The patients' blood pressure has either shot up or fallen down sharply; their old ulcers are acting up. There is not much that the puzzled doctors can do for their patients' condition. Much like the voodoo priests, they have to refer to magic and prescribe one of the two medications 'suposta' (suppositories) or 'novalgino' (Aspirin). Sometimes after I have translated the patient's complaints, I ask the doctor "novalgino" or "suposta,", "aspirin or suppositories?' And we both can't help laughing. There has never been anything else prescribed. The doctor's gentle reassuring manner convinces his patients that they have been given a good remedy for what ails them and they leave the medical office relieved.

With the money I have earned from my interpreting job, I make my first purchase, two skirts made of fine woolen fabric, one black, the other one beige. After that I have fifty dollars left in my pocket.

America is our next stop.

A Letter from Italy to my English professor

Dear Irina Aleksandrovna,

I am slowly coming back to life. The Adriatic Sea helps greatly. As I plunge into its warm water the waves hug and lull me and

I forgive life. God has created a miracle and named it The Adriatic Sea. Then he made peaches for 390 lires per pound, which is probably 39 kopecks. He has also created magnificent enormous grapes. Here is the actual size of a grape for you. Then he sprawled suntanned Italian women in colorful swimsuits all over the beach and pushed funny three rider bikes down the streets of this little town. I've already taken a ride on such a bike and tasted a three-colored ice cream, which is sold here in cones. The ice-cream cone looks like this.

I am writing this letter from Ladispoli, the little resort town located either sixty or ninety minutes away from Rome, depending on the mood of the train. The ticket to Rome is expensive and the weather is hot, so we seldom venture to Rome. Cars and bicycles are the only way of transportation here. Having been warned by the Soviet press that it is too dangerous to walk on the streets of Italy after seven o'clock, I was pleasantly surprised to see that there is practically no crime to speak of. They had recently celebrated national holidays, yet I did not see a single drunk or witnessed a single brawl. When I asked Italians what they were celebrating they told me that they were marking the middle of August. It sounded so nice – it's not the Red army Day, not the International Woman's Day, just The Middle of August. There was singing and dancing in every open cafe and on every square. Bands were playing all over the town.

It's difficult to believe that Italy has the lowest standard of living in Europe or so we are told. To my eye, Italians look quite comfortable. Every family I see has three or more offspring. I understand that here the government helps families with children. Apartments in Ladispoli are spacious and beautiful with big kitchens, bathrooms and balconies. Italians look like a crisscross between gypsies and Jews. They are short and dark with the laziness that is akin to a Russian. However, the Russian laziness is poetic in origin, while Italian laziness is that of a thief. They love to outsmart, outweigh and overcharge you. At first our immigrants didn't know how to react to this, but little by little

24

they are getting a handle on the situation. One of our men who has been overcharged while buying a chicken in the market beat the butcher on the head with the same chicken. Now every time he shows up at the market, Italians shout "Good for you, Russo!"

Italians wear bright shapeless gypsy-like clothes. We are told that Rome is considered to be a province and if we want to see real Italy we should travel to Naples, Pompeii or Venice. Alas, this is possible only for those who have brought things for sale, such as cameras, spoons and bed sheets. I brought none of those. I have some good news; I am employed. I work as a medical interpreter four hours a day.

Everything is both not as tragic and at the same time much more tragic than I anticipated it to be. The good thing is that the streets are free of crime, teenagers are well mannered, women look relaxed and satisfied, the Vatican was beautiful and I have enough money for much better food than I ate at home. The tragic thing is that immigration is like surgery and as after any surgery everything hurts. And yet if you want to live, you have to go under the knife. When I look around, I see all those sunny, smiling suntanned people who have gotten all this beauty without having to undergo any surgical intervention.

It scares me to think that I could have died and gone to heaven without seeing all this beauty.

I love you all,
Irina

AMERICA

I land in America on September 19, 1979 with $50 in my pocket
and two suitcases whose contents include:

an aluminum pot,

my grandpa's alarm clock,

two cotton tops made for me by my friend and teacher,
Professor Irina Lebedeva,

a pair of old patched up high heeled black leather boots,

a down pillow and two sheets,

a tweed winter coat,

a black woolen sweater,

two woolen skirts purchased by me in Italy,

a set of heirloom silverware from my family,

a plastic cup and a plate,

a pink nightgown,

four pairs of underwear,

a light woolen checkered blanket

and a gray silk dress.

I carry my two suitcases down the endless corridors of Kennedy Airport in New York. After going through customs we get on the bus. The bus driver, in a deep velvet voice, black as night itself announces that our first stop will be Sea Gate, Brooklyn. Up till now the only black person I saw live was that funny three-year-old on the beach in Ladispoli who entertained himself by biting the toes of sunbathers. Other than him I've seen black people only in the movies. We pass through the streets adorned by groups of identical eight story buildings which we later learn are the projects, poor people's housing. The streets are dirty, and the wind is rolling newspapers on the ground. I see a policeman with a German shepherd on a leash, straight out of Nazi Germany. Once we pass through the gates of Sea Gate, the scenery changes. Here the streets are clean. Two and three-storied houses are surrounded by bushes and bright flower gardens. I am surprised to see that the woman jogging down the street is wearing no bra. The bus grinds to a stop. We get out and I welcome the smell and sound of the ocean. When we enter a two-storied wooden house, we find ourselves in an old age home. Old folks are sitting in the cafeteria waiting for breakfast to be served. Some of them smile and wave to us, other faces are expressionless and they look at us as if they were looking through a window. I've never seen so many old people in the same place. In Latvia old folks die at home. The old age home is clean but the smell bothers me- it's an old people's smell. Once they have placed me in a room, I fall asleep instantly and sleep throughout the day. At night I get up and wander down an endless dimly lit corridor in search of a bathroom. All the doors are closed and not a sigh, or cough escapes from behind them. Only the old wooden floor is creaking under my feet. At the end of the corridor a door is wide open and there is light. An old woman in curlers is sitting regally on a high toilet like a mad queen, her arms resting on hand bars. As she sees me, the cave of her toothless mouth opens in a wide welcoming smile. Horrified, I turn around and hurry back down the corridor, followed by her shriek of laughter, "Come back, come ba-a-ack!" she is shouting. "Come ba-a-a-ck. Ha-ha-ha-ha-a-a."

The next morning each of us is handed a book of food stamps and we walk to the local supermarket called Key Food to get some food. The doors of the supermarket open by themselves but refuse to close behind me when I attempt to close them. After struggling with the doors unsuccessfully for some time I finally give up and walk away. As I look back, I see the doors close behind me by themselves. In the store I marvel at the endless shelves filled from top to bottom with rows of cans, bottles and boxes. There is even an aisle for pet food, something I have never seen before. A few shoppers are silently walking around pushing big carts and consulting some papers in their hands. I think that these must be maps of the store, which orient them to the needed aisle. How else would they be able to find their way around the huge store? We are too shy to ask where they have gotten their maps. For a long time we search for the simple staples of milk, bread, eggs and cheese. We have to adjust to the new measurements of pounds, quarts, pints and gallons instead of liters, grams and kilograms used in Europe. Walking down the aisles I marvel at the abundance of this new country. Later I learn that what I first thought to be the map of the supermarket was a sheet with all the specials in the store printed on it. When we return to Sea Gate, we have to go through a checkpoint. Out of his booth a guard views us indifferently and waves us in.

IN SEARCH OF AN APARTMENT

Every morning Fima and I leave Sea Gate in search of an apartment. His wife and daughter stay home. So far we've had no luck. Either the rent is too high or the neighborhood is too bad. The concept of a bad neighborhood we come to grips with very quickly. It means where African Americans and Hispanics live. In the Soviet Union we were taught that racism is a bad thing. That's why Russian immigrants at first seek housing in black projects. The projects located near the beaches of Coney Island have new, clean and spacious apartments. The black people living there are afraid that white tenants will bring their rents up. They assault them in the elevators. Thus, the white immigrants look for housing elsewhere.

As we are traveling in search of an apartment we meet different people to whom we ask many questions. At times I'm quite embarrassed at my inability to understand American English. Out of their mouths words roll faster than potatoes out of an overturned bucket. It's all the worse because I am an English teacher and I am traveling with my former student who becomes a witness to my humiliation. But the worst thing is watching funny programs on TV. While the audience is roaring with laughter, I don't understand a word. At the University I studied the Queen's English; I read Shakespeare and Byron, but I had never studied American English or learned the simple words like knob, screw, staple, bagel, etc. One day before work I go into a cafe and order a cup of coffee and a bagel. I mispronounce the word "bagel"; the waitress doesn't understand me. She brings me a cup of coffee only. I am too embarrassed to repeat my request and leave the cafe with my stomach growling from hunger. When a woman on the street approaches me with a question, "Do you have the time?" I don't know what she means and answer that I don't. She looks at my watch scornfully. Later I learn that she was asking me what time it was. I have to admit to myself that after studying English for over twenty years: three years with a private teacher, eleven years at a public school and six years at the University, I cannot understand the language. Not surprisingly, I say to myself, the emblem of the faculty of Foreign Languages at the Latvian State University was a parrot sitting on a dictionary, for we have learned English from the people, who have learned English from a dictionary. Neither we, nor our professors ever had a chance to speak English to a native speaker or see the country whose language we studied so studiously for six long years at the University.

All these thoughts are going through my tired mind as we are traveling on a subway to yet another place. An elderly American couple next to us starts up a conversation. Where are you from? Latvia? Searching for an apartment? Have you heard about Project ARI in Brighton Beach? They help immigrants from Europe find jobs and apartments? We're close to Brighton anyway, no harm in trying. Having thanked them for the information we get off at the next stop. Project ARI is located in a small two-storied building near the beach. On the second floor we wait for a social worker. A pleasant middle-aged woman with warm eyes comes out and introduces herself. Her name is Beba. She asks me where I am from and what my name is. "Irina Martkovich from Riga, Latvia? A-h-a, we've heard about you here." She nods. Heard about me? In New York? I am dumbfounded. She explains that her son's new friends from Latvia, the Vinniks, have mentioned to her that their friend from Riga is coming to New York. She remembered my name. She takes me into a big room divided into many tiny cubicles that looks like a beehive and is buzzing with the sounds of many human voices; one of these cubicles is Beba's. There we sit down and she teaches me how to secure myself a government job. I do as she tells me and after filling out loads of forms and going through several interviews I get the position of a secretary in an English school for Russian immigrants in Brighton Beach. I have a job... but still no apartment.

My job starts at the end of the month. In the meantime I am free to roam the new city. The subway is expensive, yet I travel to see

Manhattan. The center of the city with its old architecture, churches, cathedrals and very tall buildings is magnificent. The sight of people rushing down the streets makes me feel lonely and out of place for I have nowhere to hurry. Quite a few people are chewing on "hot dogs" as they are walking down the streets. These are hot sausages stuck in the buns of white bread sold by street vendors. The hot dogs smell deliciously. I'd like to taste one but have no money, so I unwrap the sandwich I brought from home. There being no benches in this strange city, I prop myself against the wall and eat it standing. No one is paying me any attention. Having done some window shopping on Fifth Avenue I take the B-train back to Brooklyn.

MY FIRST AMERICAN BOSS

My boss Donna, the director of the ESL (English as a Second Language) Program, is warm and friendly. Short, skinny with wiry dark brown hair, she is all sharp angles and reminds me of a cricket. Yesterday she came into the office wearing her sweater inside out. I pointed it out to her, thinking that she had made a mistake. She explained that because she owns two cats who shed fur on everything, the inside of her sweater is cleaner than the outside and that is how she wears it, the clean side out.

Donna has introduced me to many of her friends, her boyfriend Michael among them. Michael is in his late thirties, a tall Irish fellow with a lot of light frizzy hair; an engineer now an English as a Second Language Instructor. Last Friday afternoon Michael invited Alex and me over to his house on Delancey Street. Alex is a teacher in the ESL program where I am working as a secretary. He immigrated to America from Ukraine a year and a half before me. We were invited to Michael's house for five o'clock. Alex and I wondered whether we should get there at five or a little later. After some hesitation we decided to get there at five o'clock sharp. Alex met me at a subway station dressed in a dark suit and a tie as if he were headed for a funeral. When we arrived at Michael's house, and rang the bell, he was in the shower. He came out wrapped in a towel to open the door. Michael and Donna served shrimp and scallops for dinner. Neither Alex nor I had tasted this kind of seafood before. I found it delicious. Alex, on the other hand, refused to touch it. He kept watching me suspiciously. Hissing in Russian, he said, "Irina, I cannot believe that you are eating this horror." I smiled.

Donna shares an apartment with her cousin Janet in Greenwich Village. It looks as if it has been hit by a hurricane that swirled every object up into the air. Once the hurricane passed, everything fell down and remains right where it landed. Donna's sofa is like a landfill with a gorgeous long haired gray cat sitting on top of it who is benevolently observing the world of destruction and singing to himself a song of total satisfaction. I understand that here in America an apartment in such a state indicates that a free spirit dwells in it. In old times in Latvia, before hiring a worker, a perspective employer used to visit his house. He would never hire somebody who lived in an untidy house. I think this custom started the tradition of order and cleanliness in my old country. Also, for many years Latvia was ruled by Germans, who were known for their cleanliness and orderliness. Though nowadays no employers would inspect their perspective workers' homes before hiring them, apartments in Latvia are usually pretty clean. Another reason for this is that friends in Latvia are in the habit of dropping by unannounced because very few people possess phones. Obsessive cleaning is the only form of obsessive behavior I had observed in Latvia and at times this obsession is passed on to the next generation. Our old Latvian super from Brooklyn whose children were born in America, told me that he loves to eat oat cookies in his daughter's house. He makes sure he doesn't leave any crumbs on her wooden, well polished table. He demonstrated to me how carefully he extracts the cookie out of a jar, carries it straight to his mouth and carefully chews it, holding his hand under his chin. Yet each time, he said in mock desperation, when his daughter arrives home from work, she comes into the kitchen and announces to the world, "Papi had a cookie."

Job Advancement

Last week Donna got a call from a director of an ESL program in Queens who was desperate for a substitute. Knowing that I used to teach English in Latvia, she asked me if I was willing to travel all the way to Queens and teach the class there. Willing? I was delighted. After class, the students asked the director of the Queens program if I could take over their class. Having learned about this Donna offers me a class in our program. I am thrilled to be teaching again.

MY FIRST APARTMENT

Esfir Apollon is a Russian teacher from Ukraine with whom I am sharing an attic apartment in a three-storied private house in Brooklyn. We met on the plane coming to America. Like me, Esfir was traveling on her own. Very few people come from the Soviet Union without a family. So far I have met only two people beside myself who have emigrated all by themselves. When Esfir came to Brooklyn, she contacted me and asked if I wanted to share an apartment. I readily agreed.

That's how we have moved into a top floor apartment in a private house. There are three tiny rooms: one room is mine, the other one is hers and there is also a room in between. We have a bathroom with a shower but there is no kitchen, so we cook on an electric plate. I find speaking English the whole day at work exhausting. When I come home, I lie down and fall asleep. That's when Esfir comes into my room, wakes me up and asks me to help her with her English assignment. I do try to help her. However, she is clearly insane and cannot learn the language because she cannot remember a thing, which upsets her tremendously and makes her extremely bitchy. For some reason she has decided that I hold a key to her mastering the English language, but I am unable to help her. For the time being she isn't working. She is attending English classes at NYANA (New York Association for New Americans). Esfir is a tall bony woman of 47 with a long porous nose and a mop of dry dyed permed red hair, who doesn't know a word of English and has no profession. It's a difficult age at which to transplant oneself to another country whose language you don't know. There are thousands like her. Some of them go insane, others commit suicide. I have heard about a Russian poet who shot himself after the Soviet Embassy had refused to let him back into the Soviet Union.

A week ago Esfir fell down in the middle of the night and had to be taken to the hospital. We don't have a phone yet, so I woke up our downstairs neighbors who called an ambulance. Since she doesn't speak English I had to accompany her to Maimonides hospital and then walk back a distance of two miles at four o'clock in the morning through the deserted streets of Brooklyn.

Last Friday they had delivered the luggage that she had been so concerned about. Since Esfir was at the hospital, it was our landlord who accepted it. A big truck pulled up in front of the house and two tall black men dressed in green pants and yellow jackets leaped out silently like two panthers. They worked quickly and in no more than fifteen minutes carried upstairs her simple luggage - aluminum pots and pans, an iron and a rug, and even a rubber boat. In the end our landlord, a big tall bearded Orthodox Jew with payees, dressed in black, appeared in the doorway, breathing heavily as a furnace ready to explode and sweating profusely under his hat. In one hand he was holding oars for the boat, in the other an enema bag.

MY OWN APARTMENT

I found my own place through Marsha, a young woman from Lithuania who had tipped me off about an apartment in a building down the street. Finding living accommodations in New York is not easy. New Yorkers joke that if you are looking for an apartment you should look through the weekly obituaries in the Sunday *New York Times*. It was the end of the month and the tenants were moving out. I had to make up my mind in a matter of hours. I took the apartment and moved in on the same day. It happened so quickly that in between accepting the apartment and moving in, I forgot what floor it was on or its number. Having come from the country where three generations live and die in the same apartment and sometimes in the same room, I guess I got a little befuddled. My Lithuanian friend Robik who was helping me with the move looked at me in amazement and said. "I've seen many a crazy person but this is the first time that I see a gal who doesn't know where she lives."

Speaking of living accommodations in the Soviet Union, I will always remember a story about a family that consisted of a mother, father and their three daughters who all shared one room. For twenty years they were promised a bigger apartment. However, each time they were supposed to move into a new apartment, they were passed over in favor of a party member. The last time it happened the youngest daughter hung herself in the bathroom.As a rule, an apartment here is painted before a new tenant moves in, which takes no longer than two days. In my case the super Pedro, a short, bulky Spanish man in his late forties, started painting mine when I was already living there. When on the fifth day I came home and saw that he had not finished the job yet, I told my landlady that I would kill Pedro, which must have sounded pretty convincing for the next day my renovation was finished.

It was a studio apartment that consisted of one room, a kitchen and a bathroom. I had a table, three chairs, a mattress on the floor, a refrigerator and a gas stove. Yes, indeed, I did have a gas stove! Sima, a friend of mine from Riga brought me some pots, pans and dishes. Donna, my boss, presented me with a towel, a dish rack and some silverware. My friend Muriel, a chemistry teacher who volunteers as an ESL teacher in our program, brought me a tablecloth. It's mind boggling how many things one needs in order to survive. Today I have bought myself a green cotton skirt. Now I need a basin to wash it in and some detergent to wash it with. I also need an iron, a hanger and so on and so forth. There is no end to it.

A THRILLER

A young man by the name of Dan whom I met through a friend of mine has invited me to see a thriller called "Dressed to Kill". Having never seen a thriller before, I gladly accept the invitation. We meet at the movie theater where we go down the escalator. Dan buys a big paper bucket of popcorn, two large Cokes and we step into an enormous hall. The seats are not numbered, the way they are in Latvia, so we sit down in the middle of the hall.

Now, so many years later I don't remember what the thriller "Dressed to Kill" was about. Like any other thriller it must have been about somebody who was trying to kill somebody else who was trying to avoid being killed. Being a person of a balanced mind, I am not overly impressionable and not easily given to tears, yet after seeing this movie I couldn't stop crying for hours. I guess, having never seen a thriller before, I had no antibodies for this type of entertainment. "Dressed to Kill" is the one and only thriller I have ever seen. With the exception of an occasional Hitchcock I never went to see a thriller again. Dan who was both alarmed and embarrassed by my reaction never took me to the movies again.

MY SHORT BUT IMPRESSIVE CAREER AS MATA HARI

There is an International English as a Second Language conference in Detroit. Three of us, Pauline, our project director, Donna, the Director of our ESL program and I, an ESL instructor, are going there to give a panel presentation entitled "Russians are Here." This is the first time I get out of New York. To my disappointment, I don't see much of Detroit. We stay in an enormous hotel, which looks like a city within a city with many cafes, restaurants and shops, which are swarming with thousands of people. It looks and feels like being in a monstrous beehive. Our presentation attracts a sizable audience. Pauline is speaking about establishing the Center for Russian immigrants, Donna about directing the ESL program in Brighton Beach and I - about the enigmatic Russian soul. During the question-answer period people ask us many questions. "Why are there so many engineers among Russian men?" "An engineer is the most popular profession for men in Russia," I answer. "What has surprised you the most about America?" "Low level of education." They ask me to explain myself. "Knowing the US to be the leader in the world of technology, I've never expected to see so many illiterate Americans. Likewise, among teachers, I would expect to hear some conversations about new books, theater performances or concerts. But I have never heard any of that." An American teacher in the audience is deeply hurt. "I have no time for concerts," she says bitterly. "I have to pay my mortgage."

After the presentation many people approach us with questions. Among them there is a blonde blue-eyed Russian teacher in a gray business suit. Instead of introducing herself, as everybody else does, she starts interrogating me. "Is this your name on the blackboard?" "Yes, it is." "Where are you from?" Latvia. "Where in Latvia?" "Riga." "Do you have any relatives still living there?" Throughout the conversation she retains a totally expressionless face talking to her. All of a sudden my subconscious warns me to end this conversation immediately. I excuse myself. There are other people waiting to speak to me, I say. Hesitantly she steps aside. Later in the day when Pauline, Donna and I are celebrating our success in the hotel restaurant, a colleague at the next table asks me if I have gotten to meet an English teacher from the Soviet Union who came to Detroit for the Teacher's Conference. "I hope you did get to speak to her. She is going back to Moscow tomorrow morning," she says. My heart skips a beat. I know only too well that Soviet teachers are not allowed to speak to foreigners or travel out of the country to international conventions. Originally I had thought that the Russian-speaking teacher was an immigrant like me. Now I understand why I got that chilled feeling while to talking her - she was a KGB agent. At night I toss and turn. I worry about my family and what repercussions all this may have for them.

Back in New York, a former neighbor of mine, Riva, an orthodox Jewish woman stops me on the street. "Irina," she lowers her voice to a whisper, "three FBI men banged on the door of our house the other night asking for you. We told them that you had moved and we didn't know your whereabouts." The FBI is looking for me? I thanked her for this information and called the FBI the next morning. I don't believe that the FBI may be interested in my persona, and if it is not them, I would like to know who went around Brooklyn, looking for me at night. At the FBI offices I gave my name to the secretary. "I was told that three FBI men came to my former apartment looking for me." I said, "Is it true that the FBI is looking for me?" "Let me see," she said and left me waiting for a while. When she returned, at first she said no, they were not looking for me, and then she apologized and said yes, they were. We made an appointment for them to come to my new apartment the following Thursday. On Thursday they called to cancel the appointment; they couldn't make it. We agreed to meet a week later at the school in Brighton where I taught English.

This time two men dressed in dark suits came to school and sat down at desks in my classroom.. One of them looked as if he had spent a day on the beach without applying sun block. The other man in dimmed glasses was nondescript. The pink man was asking questions. When did I arrive in the USA? What was my profession in the Soviet Union? When did I move into my new apartment? I dutifully answered all his questions. In the end the pink man came up with a surprising question, "Why aren't you married?" "Should I be?" I asked him. The man was feeling ill at ease; his face got a shade redder. "These two men are no match for the well trained, highly educated and extremely intelligent KGB agents," I thought to myself, "I hope that this new country of mine does not depend on this intelligence for any serious work, or it is going to find itself in trouble." After loosening his collar, the pink man offered me his limp hand, thanked me for my time and both men departed hastily.

I often wonder if there was any connection between my conversation with the teacher from the Soviet Union and the FBI interest in my persona. Do the FBI men watch KGB agents at international events? Did they observe the woman talking to me? Was that the reason they came to question me in New York or was it just a routine check-up? I guess I'll never know the answer.

Later that year my family's apartment in Riga was ransacked by the KGB. They searched for hours but found nothing.

DREAMS OF AN IMMIGRANT

I heard about this while still in Riga. Every night thousands of Russian immigrants see the same collective nightmare. They dream that they have returned home to Russia on a visit. After hugs and celebration when the time comes for them to go back to America, something happens that prevents them from leaving the country. Right there and then I swore that I would never have such nightmares. Little did I know. For many years I would wake up in a sweat in the middle of the night. In my dream as I am about to leave Latvia, a mistake is discovered in my papers and being helpless to untangle the web of Soviet bureaucracy I am unable to leave the country.

This phenomenon of collective nightmares has been described by Ludmila Ulitzkaya in her novel "Joyful Burial." "Everybody dreamed their own variant of the same dream. Alik used to collect these dreams in a notebook under the title of "Dreams of an Immigrant." These dreams had the following structure. "I'm back in Russia, where I somehow end up in a locked room, or in a room with no doors, or in a garbage container or some other circumstances arise to prevent me from returning back to America. For instance, I lose my documents; I am put in jail... In his dream one Jewish man was even visited by his mother who tied him up with a rope."

As far as Alik was concerned, his dream was somewhat different. He arrives in Moscow and everything is bright and beautiful there. His friends are celebrating his arrival in a big apartment with many rooms that look both very familiar and neglected. There are crowds of people in there. Then the time comes to go to the Sheremetyevo airport and say good-byes which are no longer reminiscent of the old time tragic partings that were like dying and when he is about to board the plane, his old friend Sasha Nolikov appears and hands him several dogs on leashes. Those are excited dancing dogs with happy tails like pretzels and then Sasha Nolokov disappears and so do the rest of his friends and Alik has nobody to put in charge of his litter. They are finally announcing that the flight registration is coming to an end and a flight attendant comes up to him and announces that his airplane has taken off. He and his dogs stay in Moscow. And for some unknown reason it's clear that he has stayed there forever. The only thing he is concerned about is how his wife Nina is going to pay for their loft in Manhattan.

Later I learned that in other repressive regimes citizens had suffered from collective nightmares as well. In her book "Reading Lolita in Teheran" by Azar Nafisi this Turkish teacher described that in the class where she taught literature almost everyone had at least one nightmare in some form or another in which they either had forgotten to wear their veil or had not worn it at all, "and always in these dreams the dreamer was running, running away. In one, perhaps my own," she wrote, 'the dreamer wanted to run but she couldn't: she was rooted to the ground, right outside her front door. She could not run around, open the door and hide outside." Azar Nafisi tells about a ten-year-old who "had awakened his parents in horror telling them he had been having an "illegal dream". He had been dreaming that he was at the seaside with some men and women who were kissing, and he did not know what to do. He kept repeating to his parents that he was having illegal dreams.

DID BRITAIN REALLY EXIST?

Oh, how I wanted to go to Britain just to verify that the country whose language I had been studying since the age of five, actually existed, and was not a figment of my imagination.

Before the Soviets took over Latvia, my first English Teacher, Miss Velta, who used to run a private kindergarten in Riga, would travel to England each summer. Once the Soviet rule set in she could no longer leave Latvia. Fear and isolation prevented us from any contact with foreigners and every indication of other people's existence was thoroughly suppressed. At times a schizophrenic thought would cross my mind that there was no England and the whole world was just one bleak Soviet reality and they invented other countries and languages and the ever existent threat of war, so that we would work more and better for less money. And there I was at the faculty of foreign languages of the Latvian State University studying the non existent language of a non existent country and sweating over all those books and tests. It was almost to verify my own existence in this chain of falsehoods that I wanted to go to Britain.

There were some signs that other worlds did exist. Sometimes they would fail to jam a foreign radio station and we would hear voices appealing to us in Latvian and in Russian from thousands of miles away. Also in the last two years of college, we had this Canadian teacher by the name of Miss Marta, a living proof of other world's existence. Her stepfather, a member of the Canadian Communist Party, immigrated to the Soviet Union with his whole family which consisted of his wife, Diana, his step daughter, Dina, and her five year old daughter, Pam. Marta who used to work as a cashier at a department store in Canada was now transformed into a college professor by sheer knowledge of the English Language. When she played to us the musical tapes from her country, her eyes would inevitably fill up with tears. She missed Canada. Marta was small frail and had never mastered the intricate Latvian Language.

In college Marta used to teach us conversation. I remember her explaining to us the meaning of the expression "bad luck." "One day," she said, "I had just purchased this new Ford and took it out for a ride for the first time. I needed a leather bag, so I drove to my favorite department store. There being no parking space available, I left the car double-parked, ran into the department store, and got myself a beautiful, smooth, brown leather bag. The whole thing took no more than fifteen minutes. When I got out of the store there was a parking violation ticket on the windshield. Well, I decided that it was not going to spoil my mood, because it was such a warm sunny spring day and I went to another store to get myself a pair of matching gloves. I came to the store – same story, no parking space. So I left my car parked at the fire hydrant. It took me just ten minutes to get the matching gloves. And what do you think? When I got out of the store I saw another parking violation ticket on the windshield. When I came home my mother asked me if I had a nice day. "No," I answered, "I had bad luck." The story was hilarious, given the fact that she was telling it to the people for whom it would take years of hard work and scheming to accomplish what she had done in her home town in half an hour. In those times even finding a zipper in a store presented an insurmountable problem. A story goes that after a day of desperately searching for a zipper a tired shopper asked a salesperson where was the closest store where he could find one. "In Sweden," was the gloomy answer.

As a matter of fact, when my friends asked me why I decided to emigrate, I answered that I was driven to this decision by my inability to find proper footwear within the borders of my country. The largest size in women's shoes that the Soviet factories would produce was eleven, while I needed size twelve. Now just try wearing shoes a size smaller than yours for a couple of hours. It hurts? How about a lifetime of wearing them?

The closest I had ever come to going to Britain was when I was teaching at the Daugavpils Pedagogical College. I guess the bug of

Perestroyka was already in the air, for they sent a memo to our chairperson asking her to suggest a candidate for the trip to London for the purpose of professional development. This was something unheard of. The furthest that we had ever got to travel was the Moscow Library and even that was considered a blessing. After much consideration a candidate was chosen and presented to the committee. However, her candidacy was rejected. "It's because the teacher is thirty six years old," our chairperson explained." "You see, they don't send people over thirty-five abroad, for who knows how many years are left for them to live. What if they die at the age of forty. Just think of all the money spent on them for nothing." Then, either out of her naivete or out of desperation, she selected me as the next possible candidate. My candidacy was denied as well, the reasoning this time being that I had just started working on my doctorate. It may take years to complete it. Of course, nobody should travel to London without a doctorate.

In the meantime, the rumors went around that I had been chosen to go to Britain. When I entered the office the teachers surrounded me asking,

"Irina, is it true that you are going to London?"

"No," I answered.

"Why not?" You're only twenty-six, aren't you?"

"That's true, but I'm too tall."

"What?!!"

You see, one of the requirements is that the person should be no taller than five feet eight eight inches. I'm six feet. I don't fit into their weight requirements either."

They stood there for some time, studying my face for the sign of laughter. There being none, they believed me, shrugged their shoulders and left. Truth, as we know, can be stranger than fiction. I did get to go to Britain about five years later. But this is another story.

MUSEUM OF MADAME TUSSAUD

I sacrificed everything for my desire to see Great Britain; my friends, my family, my books in a cozy little room on Friedrick Engels Street in Riga, Latvia, and my future as an English Professor of the Red Banner Latvian State University, all of this so that I could find out that Britain does exist and that everyone is alive and well in that part of the world.

I emigrated to the United States, where I got married to an American by the name of Bruce, and from there we both took a trip to Britain. Seeing the United Kingdom and its capital was like looking at three – dimensional illustrations in a text book. Dutifully we went to the tower, Big Ben, Picadilly Circus and Hyde Park. But it was with a very special feeling that I set out to see the famous Wax Museum of Madame Tussaud.

When I was a child of seven, I studied English under the guidance of Miss Velta. It was then that I read a book about two blond Latvian school children, Valdis and Velta who went to England with their parents for a summer vacation. Just like that, their mom and dad took them to London for the month of July. It was a pre-Soviet publication, of course, depicting a time when people traveled freely and meat, bread, and comfortable footwear were in abundance. Of all the places that Valdis and Velta visited in London, I was most fascinated reading about the Museum Of Madame Tussaud.

It said that Madame Tussaud came to England from France and founded there a wax museum which became famous. Somewhere down the line there was a fire in the museum. The figures' arms, feet, and heads were floating in the stream of melted wax. Later the museum was restored. And that's where Bruce and I were going that morning.

When we arrived at the Museum of Madame Tussaud there was already a long line of people waiting at the entrance. As the line started moving on, we finally found ourselves in the little hall. I saw the stairs that were described in the book and looked for the wax figure of a guard. The guard was there, leaning forward, looking like a real thing, watching the line of people who came to the museum. I decided to play a trick on Bruce and asked him to go to the guard and find out the hours of the museum. He dutifully departed. I saw him approach the guard and ask a question. The guard did not pay any attention to him. Bruce repeated his question, but the man did not even move. I saw Bruce go through a predictable reaction of surprise, annoyance and frustration which I knew was bound to end in a fit of anger. Luckily before Bruce had reached the final stage, he became conscious of people's laughter behind his back, realized his mistake and sheepishly retreated back in line.

This incident has bullied him for developing deep respect towards the talent of the great Madame Tussaud, and he was determined to compensate for his initial mistake by devoting his undivided attention to every wax figure in the museum. First, he would carefully examine the figures face through the thick lenses of his glasses, then he would perform a little dance consisting of one step forward and two steps back while taking in the whole figure. And as the final stage, he would look for the plaque with the figure's name and title.

After the first three halls I realized that the museum was boring me to death. I quickly went forward, hoping to reach the end, but it was no where in sight. The rooms were dimly lit to make the characters more convincing and life-like. And they were. Very. I saw the Royal Family, Margaret Thatcher, and members of her cabinet, Pope John II, Pablo Picasso, and all the famous stars and murderers. I went through a long corridor that connected me to yet another room, where I leaned on the barrier on which more wax figures were propped. I was totally exhausted. My feet hurt. I looked around, wax figures dressed in everyday clothes, looked frighteningly real. If ever Bruce reached this point, I would plead with him to leave the museum. In vain did I peer into the long corridor hoping for his tall figure to emerge out of its semi darkness. Instead, a little fat man, hooked to a set of cameras and camera equipment rolled out of it. He was puffing heavily, sweating profusely and constantly moping his forehead with a big handkerchief.

My glance was still pinned to a corridor when I became aware that now the little man was rolling around me searching for something. Slowly I realized that he thought that I was yet another wax figure and was looking for the plague with my name. It was when he was focusing his camera on me, searching for the perfect angle that I moved. The little man grabbed his camera and pressed it to his chest in sheer terror, then realized his mistake, stepped back, frantically apologized both in French and in English and ran away as quickly as possible.

Irina At The Museum Of Madame Tussaud With The Wax Doll Of A Soldier

LETTERS FROM HOME

When I came to New York I was surprised to find that the people who felt lonely could rent a pet per diem, and those in need of advice or human connection could rent a friend for an hour. The friend did not come cheap and was called "a therapist". Most of my American acquaintances, called baby boomers, never spoke of their families. It made me wonder if they had emerged out of a test tube instead of a womb. They were brave and independent; they were nobody's responsibility and assumed no responsibility for anyone else. Later I learned that all of them were indeed a product of a human conception and came into this world with a full set of parents, siblings, aunts, uncles and cousins who had somehow gotten lost along the way. Yet they never turned back to see what had happened to their relatives or questioned why they were so completely alone and unattached in this vast universe. As a rule, their marriages failed and their relationships were temporary. The only person they desperately depended on was their therapist, who for what seemed to be an exorbitant sum of money, would spend an hour a week listening to their troubled selves. After baby boomers came "Generation X". Generation X children were brought up either in a two income family or by a single mother who was absent in body when at work and in spirit when she was back home. In essence their parents were always being too tired and exhausted, and thus, the children had never experienced living in a family. Many of them were referred to as latchkey children for they walked around with a key on a string around their neck. Eventually, as they were growing up, they did develop a semblance of a family, which consisted of a circle of close friends. Speaking of this phenomenon in his article "Oral Histories," published in the Bomb magazine, Marc Ribot called them "reinvented families" and said that they grew out of the social fragments of New York life. Those who belonged to such a "reinvented family" maintained with its members the kind of relationship that their parents did not have with their own families; they kept in touch and helped each other religiously. On the other hand, they were often quite reserved, cold and at times even hostile with the people outside their "reinvented family". The present generation, by the way, is playfully referred to as "Generation X-large" on account of its extremely overweight young people. By now the family structure has disintegrated and many young people have organized themselves into gangs.

Of all the earthly possessions I had left in Latvia, I missed my friends the most. I did miss my family, but I missed them more in a biological than psychological sense, for mine was not a supportive or loving family. To tell you the truth, when I imagine that long tunnel through which I'll have to travel to the other side where all my relatives will gather to welcome me to the after world, I start wandering if there is an alternate route. Separation from my friends, however, was the cause of almost physical pain, all the more so because at the time we could not even maintain our correspondence. When I made my decision to leave the Soviet Union, I became the enemy of the people and it was too dangerous for my friends to maintain any contact with me. They could lose a promotion or even a job if it was discovered that they corresponded with an emigre. However, a couple of them had some family members to whose address I could write. Those were old retirees whom the Soviet political system could no longer hurt.

I maintained contacts with my friend Sandra through her parents who lived away in another town. She was a lovely woman in her late thirties with a sparkle in her eyes. She was recently divorced and lived with her anemic twelve-year old daughter, Lena who looked like a sprout and loathed to study, which was all the more regrettable, since both of her parents were teachers. Her father, Pyotr, Sandra's former husband, taught The History of The Communist Party at a local college. Sandra, a high school English teacher herself, would often look at her daughter, and say with a deep sigh," My Lenushka (the tender form of the name Lena) is neither Newton nor Lobachevsky." During the two and a half years that I spent in Daugavpils, teaching English at the Pedagogical Institute, Sandra and I became friends. We lived in the same apartment building and spent long hours chatting over coffee in her tiny kitchen, taking long walks in a nearby forest, exercising in the Palace of Culture which in the Soviet Union was the equivalent of a local "Y" in America. I've kept all the letters written to me by her and her mother. Here they are.

LETTERS FROM SANDRA AND HER MOTHER

January,1980

Dear Irina,

When we finally received your long awaited letter I forwarded it to Sandra right away. Don't be surprised that I am writing to you, and please don't let her know about it.

Sandra is very lonely. Her relationship with Lena is strained. She has no friends left except for Zoya. Everybody else has emigrated. My husband and I are not ready to leave for America. My health is getting worse with each and every day. I have gone through a lot in my life. You know that I am a Holocaust survivor, don't you.

Lena doesn't listen to her mom at all. She doesn't study, skips classes and gets bad grades. At times she is so rude with her mom that they end up not speaking for weeks. As you may know, Lena is the dearest person in my life, but she behaves as if she didn't need anybody. Who knows, maybe it's just the stage she is going through [on April 30 she turned sixteen] or maybe she has been affected by all the screaming and fighting that took place prior to her parents' divorce. One thing is clear to me, Sandra's life is very difficult. I would like to be of some help to her, but I see that there is nothing I could do for my daughter. Lena's father shows no interest in her whatsoever. Sandra works all week through, with no days off. Lena is a big girl now and needs many things. Sandra is still young and can't give up on her life either. That's why I am appealing to you, Irina. If you think that there is a way to improve her sad lot, please let her know about it. She won't listen to us. You are the only person whose opinion she respects. I feel so bad.

Our son has invited us to America and my husband desperately wants to join him. He has gotten sick over this; his blood pressure has shot up. He has become very nervous and is suffering from insomnia. I am torn apart. He won't leave Latvia without me and I cannot leave without Sandra.

Our son lives in Oakland. He still has only a temporary job, and yet they have already bought a car and a Japanese color TV. Unfortunately, he does not speak English for he was unwilling to study the language here. Now he is attending the English language courses at night. His wife Sima isn't working either. She is also studying the language. They get by on Social Security compensation of $500 a month. They write to us that the climate is good there. Sima's parents are getting ready to join them. As you know my son and daughter-in-law have two children; we miss our grandchildren desperately.

Please write to us about your life in America. Our lives here are so sad, bleak and uneventful. My husband is sending you his regards. If I feel OK in May we'll go to see Tamara. She visited us on March 8. Lena isn't as fresh with us, but this is not good enough for me. I want her to be the way she is with us with everybody else, including her mom. I can't tell you how I feel for Sandra. I am so afraid she won't last long under the circumstances.

OK, enough of this. You'll get tired of my complaints. My husband Boris and I are sending you our best wishes.

Sincerely, BI.

April 1, 1980

Hello, dearest Irina,

I am so glad to have received your letter. For the reasons I'd rather not disclose right now I couldn't answer your first one right away. I am so happy that you have written me again without waiting for my response.

Your letter has been read by the whole city of Daugavpils. All those who love you are delighted that you finally seem to be settling down. We all reminisced about you, Lera, Zoya, Harry and so many others. Please write to us in greatest detail about your life and all your new friends and acquaintances.

There are no changes on this side of the border. Our life with Lenushka is pretty much the same. We are still struggling with math. She hasn't turned into Newton or Lobachevsky. Now she wants to study languages. At first I tried to talk her out of it but then decided that it may be an incentive, and she would pay more attention to her studies. She has joined college prep courses. I tried to steer her towards becoming a librarian thinking that this profession would be closer to her nature. Much to my regret she doesn't want even to hear about it.

My life is serene and I started gaining weight. So far I put on four kilograms. I often think about you. Now that you are gone, there's nobody to inspire me to lose weight. I think that you must have slimmed quite a bit. I work a lot, twenty-six hours a week altogether. Sometimes I also travel to Riga or Kaunas as a tourist guide. We have finally managed to purchase a color TV on time.

Oh, I almost forgot to tell you that I had spent eighteen days in

Bulgaria. The first six days we traveled around the country. The next twelve days we spent in the region of Sluchev Breg on the Black Sea. The weather was wonderful and I got a good sun tan. When I came back home, the weather here was so cool that I had to don my heavy clothing right away and couldn't even flaunt my fabulous suntan. Now I am white all over again.

The other day Katya came over with her kids and her newly acquired elder terrier. The dog is so cute. They also bought a summerhouse last year and now are spending all their free time fixing it. I heard that Valera has gotten a big promotion.

Zoya visits me weekly. She has no news and no friends, except me. I am glad when she comes over. You know how I love to sip coffee in my kitchen in the company of my friends but I am not the right company for her. I tried to explain to her that she should be visiting places where she could meet some perspective bachelors but she doesn't seem to understand me.

Well, this is the end of my first letter to you. Be well, my dear.

Love, Sandra.

October, 1980

Hello, dear Irina,

Excuse my bad handwriting but it is difficult to write while sitting in bed propped by the pillows. Brace yourself. This is going to be a sad letter.

I got sick right after the New Year. At first they thought that I had Bodkin's disease because I had developed yellow complexion and placed me in the infectious ward. Then they changed their diagnosis and operated on me. The operation lasted three hours *and twenty minutes during which they removed my gallbladder. Three weeks later I was transferred to a Kiev clinic where a professor spent two and a half hours operating on my liver. It's been almost two months since the operation. I have just started walking around the house. I am very weak. Different doctors visit me often but without any results. The worst thing is that my complexion has become frighteningly yellow and I am very thin. I've lost sixteen kilograms and have only fifty kilograms left. I am not as concerned about my weight as I am about my complexion. Doctors say that this condition may last for a year. I hope that I won't remain this way forever.*

I was reading your letter and crying. I think of you often. I remember how we used to drink coffee in my kitchen, the nice atmosphere that you used to create in spite of all the hardships that you were going through at the time.

People show me a lot of care, my school is very involved too but of course the main burden is on my mom's shoulders. She amazes me. She's been with me since day one of my sickness. I wonder where her strength comes from. Zoya is also a big help. Katya however has not showed up even once since my return from Kiev. I wonder if she is coldhearted or maybe she is just trying to separate herself from other people's misfortunes.

And how are you, my dear friend? Are you going to travel anywhere this year? Write to me about your American boyfriend and all your new friends and acquaintances. Lenusha is taking her exams. As always, she doesn't break a sweat. She is sending you her regards.

Love, Sandra.

March, 1981

65

Hello, Dear Irina,

Let you live a long life. This is probably my last letter to you. After my operation I felt better for a while. I even started walking around the house. However, cirrhosis is a treacherous disease. Soon after I developed fever. My temperature has stayed at 38 degrees for eleven weeks. I survive on my mom's energy and my brother's money. Sometimes I get blood transfusions but every time it becomes more and more difficult to get through one. I weigh forty-five kilograms and have very little strength left. I am praying for an easy, pain free end.

My tears are for Lenushka. She has no idea what life is all about. She will stay alone in a big, freshly painted apartment that her father cannot wait to lay his hands on. He has re-married and complains bitterly about the lack of living space. I know that her uncle won't abandon her; I am also leaving her some money but this all will go up in smoke for she has her dad's careless nature. She is very naive and doesn't know how to communicate with people. Her grandparents love her to death but she has no respect for them. I am terrified of leaving such a person alone in this world. She will never graduate from college because she doesn't want to study. I have no idea what she is going to do in life, whose advice she'll be listening to. This tortures me day and night.

Farewell, Irochka. I'll ask Lenushka to inform you of my death. Remember me, remember my kitchen where we spent hours chatting over cups of coffee, and remember how we met in Riga after you had left Daugavpils, in other words all the good stuff.

Farewell,
I kiss you, Sandra

This was Sandra's last letter. I wrote to her address several times. There was no answer. Thus I have always felt that there has been no closure… that is up till now. Tamara, I have found no substitute for you in my life. I love you dearly, I miss you a lot. I hope you can hear me wherever you are and I pray that you have finally found peace, I am still searching for mine.

LETTERS FROM MY FAMILY

Ever since I left Latvia my family had spent their afternoons in Riga glued to the TV screen in the hope that they would see my face in the crowds of New Yorkers shown during the international news. It never happened. Instead, they were shown the Soviet propaganda films. Any hurricane, flood in a capitalist country would immediately get an extensive coverage on TV accompanied by photos. Belonging to the Socialist block automatically exempted them from any natural disaster. I would think that that was also the reason for their under reporting the worst in the world nuclear disaster in Chernobil. There was no precedent for that type of disclosure. Many people report that the first sign of trouble were dozens of children covered by white sheets that parents were putting on the planes in the Kiev airport.

Soviet journalists always filmed New York in bad weather. How often did I read in my mother's letters. "Yesterday I watched New York on TV. It was rainy and the city looked quite unappealing."

The following letter I received from my father.

Many greetings, my daughter,

The other day they showed the streets of New York on TV. It was raining hard. Right on the street the homeless were eating and sleeping wrapped in cellophane sheets. How terrible.

In spite of our quite low standard of living you can see nothing of the kind. Such hopelessness is awful.

We know nothing of your circumstances and we are worried all the more because there is nothing we can do to help you.

Write to us in greatest detail about your life there.

Wishing you the best,
Dad

And, of course, there was a joke about rain.

A joke. There is a party meeting at which the horrors of capitalism are described to the

audience in the hope of preventing Soviet citizens from emigrating.

"The capitalist world is ruthless," a party member warns the audience "There is high unemployment, crime and hunger, there are people living on the streets, but worst of all," he continues, "worst of all is the climate. You see it always rains there. It's raining when you get up in the morning; it's raining when you go out for lunch and come home from work; and it's raining when you go to bed at night." The face of an old Jew by the name of Abram Abramovich sitting in the front row reflects the process of deep contemplation. "I can tell by looking at you, Comrade Abramovich, that you are in deep thought," says the party member. "Would you please share your thoughts with the audience." Abram Abramovich gets up, scratches his bald freckled head and sighs, "Comrade Ivanov," he says, "I am considering whether I should pack my umbrella or leave it here."

MY SISTER'S LETTERS
were short and cold. More about her later.

MY MOTHER'S LETTERS

Usually followed the same pattern. As a rule they started with the weather forecast. Then the list of do's and don'ts followed. For example if I wrote that I was studying for a driver's test, my mother would respond with a warning, "Don't buy a car!" Several clips from the Soviet periodicals would be included in that letter. They would start with a joke like this one. "A policeman stops a motorist on a highway. "Have I been driving too fast, officer?" inquires the motorist. "No, not at all. It's just that you've been flying too low." The joke would be followed by a historical record. "The first traffic accident in Great Britain occurred in August of 1896 when a car driving at a speed of six kilometers per hour hit a pedestrian." This would be followed by a clip containing an ominous warning, "According to the World Health organization, the death toll from car accidents shares the first place with such life threatening diseases as heart attacks and cancer. Every year two hundred fifty thousand people die in traffic accidents and about seven million are badly injured."

MY FATHER'S LETTERS

were usually very concise. In his many years of working as a chief marine engineer on Baltic ships he had acquired the habit of writing concise messages in the ship journals. The following was the longest letter I had ever received from my father.

My dear daughter,

Lately you've been complaining that my letters are too short and "sound pretty much like a weather forecast." Well, here is a long and informative letter, for a change.

Since day one this New Year, which we hoped would bring us some relief from our recent misfortunes, has showered us with new disasters instead. It all started on January 1, when I suffered my first heart attack. That morning I started experiencing severe chest pains, and your mother helped me into bed. The pain had diminished during the day but never went away completely. At night Taya called an ambulance. A kind lady doctor arrived and after giving me an injection called for a cardiogram to be performed. Even though the cardiogram didn't reveal anything alarming, she recommended a specialist be called in from the clinic. The specialist arrived the next morning, but couldn't find anything wrong with me either. Yet he ordered another cardiogram to be performed on Tuesday and told me to stay in bed until then. On Tuesday a nurse performed another cardiogram after which we received a call from the clinic. They told us that I was on the brink of a stroke and that the ambulance was on its way. The ambulance came and they took me to the hospital on a stretcher. There they started all kinds of stroke preventative treatments. The cardiogram performed a couple of days later did not reveal anything troublesome. To be on the safe side, they continued with their preventative treatments for both a stroke and high blood pressure. You see, right before the New Year my blood pressure shot up to 230/120. It is then that your mother expressed her regret that we couldn't even celebrate in a proper fashion our last New Year together. Those were her exact words "our last New Year together."

On the morning of January 23, a nurse brought in a tray of anti-depressants and ordered me to take them. After that Abik came into the room and told me that your mom had passed away that morning. They helped me dress and sent me home in a cab. In the meantime, Taya was on her way back from Warsaw. Her train was supposed to arrive at 10:20. No one was home the morning your mom died, except for Vladimir, our distant relative from Warsaw, a quiet, well-mannered and educated young man. When he came into the bedroom your poor mom was lying on her bed, her body still warm. She must have tried to get up, but fell on the bed and died. Poor Vladimir was so shook up; he didn't know what to do. Luckily Abik came by that morning and took charge.

Your mom passed away like a saint, without any suffering. For many years she had been plagued by high blood pressure and lived

in fear of being paralyzed by a stroke. She didn't want to suffer,
nor did she want to be a burden to her family. She always prayed
for a quick death. As it often happens with patients like her, in
the last two years of her life her health was deteriorating with
every day. In the end it became difficult for her to walk. Most of
the time she just sat there and worried about all of us, waited for
your letters, waited for your sister to come home at night.

Thank God for Taya who did everything that had to be done.
Also, my co-workers turned out to be very helpful. We buried
your mom at a new cemetery, right across the lake, far away from
the city. I ordered for her a burial service with a priest and
candles. Even though she was not a religious woman, since her
early childhood spent in a rural area, she had retained the
memory of the beauty of a church service. In essence she was a real
Christian, brave, kind and responsive, the kind of a woman who"
would stop a galloping horse and enter a burning hut." As the
priest was praying for her soul and asking God to forgive her sins,
both intentional and unintentional, I was thinking that she had
neither. She was not a woman of many words, yet she was always
caring, kind and hard working. Now we have been orphaned.

The day before her death I called her from the hospital and in
her already weak voice she told me that she had received two
letters from you. I am glad that you have managed to brighten
up her last day with the news of your marriage. I congratulate
you on your marriage, my oldest daughter.

After the burial, according to the custom, we all sat down at the
table with food and drink. I have been crying for three days
since. Tears are trickling down my face and there is nothing I can
do about it. Luckily, I have been given sick leave until Tuesday. I
am crying for your mother. We've been together since World
War II. She died one month before her 64th birthday.

The shoes you've sent her are still traveling on their way home.
The ones you sent me have finally arrived. I put them on and

they are as comfortable as a dream. Thank you so much.

The musical card that you have sent us must have gotten lost in the mail.

Please accept our congratulations on receiving your American citizenship.

Taya has proven to be a very caring and understanding daughter for which I am so grateful. I feel lost and helpless as if all my resources were coming to an end. You know, she told me that as a child, she was terrified of the flying airplanes. Isn't it strange how children inherit their parents' fears? Your mom and I were bombed all throughout the WWII and the horror that we had experienced then was passed over to the innocent child.

Love,
Dad

P.S. I don't know the customs of your new homeland but here when a young man becomes a part of the family, he introduces himself to its members. I would be glad to receive a letter from your husband. My father wrote the letters to his son-in-law, my American husband Bruce, in English. When my father was younger, he knew English quite well. In his forties he translated from English a book on ship engineering. By the time the letters to his son-in-low were written, he had forgotten much of his English. His letters must have been edited by my sister Taya, also an English major.

_____

July, 28, 1985

Dear Bruce,

We have a pleasure of getting a new member of our family the size of about two meters and the weight of 90 kilograms. Your particular presentation of your genealogical table is very kind on your part and confirms your full respectability. We are glad to receive a new son in our orphaned family. Accept our faithful congratulations on your wedding. We wish that your desires and hopes be fulfilled. I was very happy to learn that you were pleased with my wedding present. It appears to me that if you get acquainted with our ancestry, it will help you to enter our family. To put it frankly, I believe that you are in no need of such a present. But if it is interesting to you, I shall continue to send you the survived photos.

As to Irena's great grandfather, my mother's father, he was a very healthy, strong and energetic man who started from nothing and was able to make himself a noticeable person among his own folk. He had nine daughters and one son. My father was his favorite son-in-law.

Do pass my compliments to your own mother. I wish her a quick recovery.

I wish you success in your business. As they say in the East, a good daughter will bring a son into the house. I am very happy to acquire you for such a son but I am sorry that I can't embrace you, as it should be done.

Your father,
Anatol.

October, 19, 1985

Dear Bruce,

I was very pleased to receive your letter from September 15. It's very good that both of you are living in friendship and are glad with each other.

I feel satisfactory and after a week I shall return home from the sanatorium, which is situated at the Riga beach.

Now I shall try to tell you about Irina mother's side of the family. Her mother was born in a small Siberian village situated near the Taiga, located so near the forest that in the winter bears would come out to them. She was a descendant of an ancient family. Her father was a Cossack and her mother was a noblewoman from a ruined noble family. She grew up in a village and was such an inexperienced girl that during her first visit to the city she lost all the cash for the train ticket home. She was a very reserved, close-tongued woman with a great sense of dignity and at the same time good natured and responsive. We met during the war in the little Black Sea port Tuapse. It was a very hard time for both of us. She had very little food. I was in a much better situation thanks to the marine ration. I was not hungry.

My wife's mother died during the war, her father worked at a coal mine and died after the war, her brother Stepan has died this year and her sister Irene lives in the Ukraine and her health is also bad enough. As you can see our family has become small. If I can find the photo of the relatives on my wife's side, I shall make copies and send them to you. Excuse my English. Receive my best wishes,

Your father,
Anatol.

August 08, 1991

Hello, Irene and Bruce,

Father became sick on March 18. He spent his last two days at the hospital. It was a trombone of one of the main blood vessels that supply the brain. He did not understand that he was dying, thank God. He asked if there were any letters from you on March 22, while still being able to talk. On Wednesday, March 25 he understood nothing when I came to see him in the morning and was gone by night.

Annie and I are all right. She is attending a kindergarten. I am starting to work. Influenza seems to have come to an end this year without visiting us. I hope that both of you are all right and healthy.

Bye, N & AM.

Irina's Mother

Irina's Father

Irina's Paternal Grandmother

Irina's Paternal Grandfather

MY TEACHERS

In my days the system of education in Latvia was very different from the one that presently exists in the United States. Here, if a student experiences some problems, a teacher sends him or her to a counselor, a description of the problem in hand. In Latvia these problems were resolved between a student and a teacher, without any outside intervention. Our teachers were our confidants, counselors, mentors. We could always ask them for help, advice or meet with them for a chat. We knew their phone numbers; we were invited over; we were introduced to their families. Very few American students get a chance to connect with their professors in this way. All the teachers at the college where I am teaching English as a Second Language are adjuncts and have no office hours. After work we rush to other jobs to make money for our mortgage and medical insurance and have no time to speak even to each other. Most of us don't know their colleagues' names. The Adjunct Office, which occupies the space of nine by six feet, is not suitable for a conversation; besides, there is always somebody else in the room. Instead of spending time between the classes in the adjunct room, I prefer to stay in my car. There I pour myself a cup of tea out of my thermos, put back my seat, turn on the radio and close my eyes. After a while I stopped parking my car in the same spot between the classes because my students would gravitate to my car for a chat. I needed my rest between the classes. In Riga I was much more fortunate than my own students are. While studying at the Faculty of Foreign Languages, I met three professors with whom I maintained close contacts long after I graduating from the University and even after emigrating from Latvia. They were Tamara Zalite, Irina Lebedeva and

Anita Nachischione. I lost touch with Irina Lebedeva after she had immigrated to Israel. Tamara Zalite died from a stroke. With Anita Naciscione I maintain contacts with to this day. We exchange letters, E-mail and meet on those rare occasions when she visits New York in the capacity of an interpreter. Tamara and Irina were at my farewell party and came to the railway station to see me off when I was leaving Latvia. I still keep one of the two tops that Irina had sewn for me when I was leaving Latvia. Being a party member, Anita couldn't come over openly to say her good-byes. She came alone, under the cover of the night to do so.

TAMARA

Tamara was a very colorful person. She was a woman who was small in stature, but big in spirit. Just being in her presence was a tonic. In her youth Tamara and her brother Joe went to London to get their education. Tamara studied dance and languages; Joe studied science. When Latvia became Soviet and Joe made a decision to return home, Tamara followed him. In Latvia she became a teacher of English literature at the Faculty of Foreign Languages of the Latvian State University. Her brother became a nuclear scientist. During the Stalin times Tamara was imprisoned and sent to Siberia. After Stalin's death she was rehabilitated and returned to Riga, where she resumed her teaching position at the Latvian State University. After I emigrated, we maintained our correspondence. Here is one of her letters.

Tamara's Letter

May 24, 1980

It's been ages since I got your nice little letter (the one with Easter eggs) – and I have been thinking of you time and again ever since, but writing comes hard if one is in a wrong frame of mind. It is wonderful to hear you in a major key, the REAL Irene. And it must be wonderful to feel happy at your job, and work with nice people who treat you with respect and sympathy. I have none of this; it is getting worse rather than better. So is our weather. My God, what a spring! They were heating until yesterday, and it is either wind or rain or both, with little patches of fog in between. Like in Macbeth ......

What could I tell you at such a distance? From one of your friends – a very attractive young woman, a cosmetician, if I am not mistaken, I heard that your sister got married. Your friend Sandra has become the sixth wife of Janis L., the "anti-Shakespearian" you must remember and I am really sorry about this. She seems like a nice kid, and he is not nice at all. But who can tell what's good or bad for another? Irina is still where you left her and I see her very rarely nowadays. I don't know why it is that she is so busy, but she always is, and is rarely at home. Her daughter seems to be really married now and perhaps she is happier. I can't visualize Irina's life, she is always vague, as you know, but she looks nice, and all right now. There was a period when she was all gray, and had pains in her joints and suffered. But the last time I saw her she was her usual self. Impenetrable, of course.

And you live on fruit and are slim. How lovely, and how I'd have liked to see you. Perhaps you'll send me a picture one day? Send me more bits of your new English; it amuses us. By us I mean Joe, of course, who sends you his best and who is as sweet and nice and unique as ever. Thank God for him. I would die without him. Although it takes a lot to die, as the measure of human endurance is unfathomable. You've done the right thing, and I hope and pray to have only letters from you that fall in with the latest I have received. Do answer soon, don't imitate me. I suppose you have gathered that I'm not exactly in the brightest of moods... That's why I think I had better stop here and leave the rest for both your intuition and a subsequent letter that may or may not materialize soon.

Much love to you. We remember you with pleasure – and I, with a mixture of a keen pang in my heart that feels almost physical. It's so strong.

Once more – love and kisses! Write!

Love,
Tamara.

"Her daughter seems to be really married now, and perhaps she is happier." Since only Jews could emigrate from the Soviet Union in those times, there were many marriages of convenience. There was a saying: "A Jew is not a luxury, he is just a mode of transportation." Irina's daughter got married to a Jewish man in the hope that this would help her emigrate. When for some reason it didn't happen, the marriage was annulled and she got married for real.

My Letter to Tamara

Dear Tamara,

So much time has passed since I last wrote to you. Let me recollect here what has happened in my life since Easter. There was a transit strike in New York during which I stayed in Muriel's house. Muriel is a retired chemistry teacher who volunteers at our program as an ESL teacher. She drove me to work and back to her house while the strike lasted. Her husband Morris is a dentist. They have three children who are all in colleges now and none of them lives at home, so Muriel and Morris are kind of lonesome. And that's how I came to benefit from their attention. They took me to the theater, a Chamber Orchestra performance, to the Brooklyn Botanical Gardens, and to Chinese, Italian and the Ukrainian restaurants. They have also introduced me to their entire family. It was really great! I wished that the strike would never end.

Among other things to be mentioned is my trip to a beautiful town of East Hampton on Long Island with Donna, Michael, Dorothy and a large white dog Leo. We collected clams on the seashore that looked painfully Baltic, then cooked and ate them. This is the first time I tasted clams and they were delicious. We also went to a Picasso's exhibition and the beautiful paintings I saw there will stay with me forever.

I am taking a Fellini course at The New School. The first film they showed us was La Strada and even though I had already seen it I enjoyed it very much.

It's June and in addition to strawberries and blueberries, mango and kiwi fruit have now appeared in fruit and vegetable markets. This abundance of fruit is such a pleasant novelty for me. I have moved into a new apartment which I don't share with anybody, it's entirely my own. The school where I work has been filmed for a TV program. I smoked marijuana (no reason to get concerned, for I didn't like it). Every day brings something new, so my pain eases little by little and my nightmares have almost disappeared. My American friends keep telling me that I started looking like an American lady. I am much more relaxed and have even regained some of my beauty, which I thought I had lost forever. I've changed so much that my former friends and acquaintances recognize me on the street with difficulty.

You have asked me for the 'bits of my new English'. Here they are. In this country the English language changes all the time. Recently when I questioned my boss Donna if one can say, "Do you have the time?", meaning "Do you know what time it is?" She answered no, you can't. Yesterday when we were sitting on the bench in Prospect Park, a woman came up to us and asked, "Do you have the time?" Donna was very surprised. Some of the language is being corrupted by immigrants. For instance, a phrase "Long time no see," has firmly established itself American English and means, of course, I have not seen you in a long time. I think it is Chinese immigrants who came with this particular phrase. But this is the beauty of English-no matter how you corrupt the grammatical structure of a sentence-you will still be understood.

The school year is over and at a party I got the biggest compliment ever. An American teacher of Polish descent overheard me speaking Russian to one of my ESL students and asked me where I had learned the Russian language so well. "I speak some Russian too," she said, "but it is a far cry from yours." I was very flattered that she didn't guess I was from the Soviet Union.

My cousin Vita gave my address to her friend Robik, who had also recently emigrated from Lithuania. He visited me once. The next time he wanted to drop by, he realized that he had forgotten his address book at home. He remembered the street and the apartment building, but not the floor that I lived on. So he asked the man who happened to be my next-door neighbor if a Russian young lady lived in the apartment next to his. "No," the man said. " An American girl lives here. A Russian lady lives on the fourth floor." He was referring to Masha, a Lithuanian friend of mine. So thanks a lot, you've taught me good English.

Well, this is all the news that's fit to print.

Please keep in touch.

Love, Irina.

During the last years of her life, Tamara found surviving at the faculty of Foreign Languages of the Latvian State University particularly difficult. She also was becoming too weak physically. She was too old to stand on long food lines and thus couldn't get proper nutrition. She had a stroke, was paralyzed and robbed of her speech, the one quality, which made her truly magnificent. Tamara died alone in her apartment, unable to call for help.

Irina's Teacher, Tamara

ANITA

Anita is a talented professor who to this day teaches at the University of Latvia. As students we adored her. She taught conversation. Many times we would call her at home and beg her to give us a class in her apartment instead of our classroom. She never refused. Her apartment located next to a church was filled to the brim with foreign books and dictionaries. When I was no longer her student, I ran into a problem while working on my course paper. Many times Anita invited me over and helped me with the paper. Throughout her life Anita has maintained an amazing level of energy. While raising her daughter on her own, she earned her P.H.D., which to this day is considered to be a humongous accomplishment in Europe. To earn a P.H.D here in America one needs to possess an average intelligence, diligence and money. What happens to a person after he or she receives a P.H.D. is nobody's concern. In America you may see a P.H.D. working at a gas station. Earning a P.H.D. in Europe is extremely difficult. However, once the degree has been earned, the person is basically set for life. They make sure that you have a job. Anita has also spent some time studying in Great Britain. She's been to the States a few times as an interpreter and once came to a conference. Each time we met and enjoyed each other's company. Here are some of Anita's letters.

Anita's Letters

March 15, 1991

Riga

Dear Irene,

*I have come home safely and, thank God, there is no more
shooting! The situation seems to have become a little bit more
stable, touch wood. The advisory pole on March 3 gave excellent
results when 74% of all the people who went to the poles (the
participation was about 84%) voted for an independent Latvia.
Even Daugavpils with only 13% of Latvian population voted
51% for independence.*

*There is a new development. There is an hour of CNN news in
English every day from 5 to 6 P.M. that includes a weather
forecast of the world. So I've been off to watch the weather in the
NY area. Of late you have been having rainstorms and
snowstorms. That's the only thing I know about you, I am afraid.
In this area we only had some two weeks of cold weather but I
haven't been freezing. The new coat I've purchased in NY is
excellent! Both warm and light. Even my mom likes it and she is
very strict in her demands. Judy's boots are perfect too. She puts
them on only in good weather. When the weather is bad she is
ready to wear shoes. She is working on her annual paper (The
Concept of Love from Augustine's Works and Classical Philosophy
in General). She has translated a twenty page article from
Latvian into English on Phenomenology. It will be published in
the US and the name of the translator will be mentioned. Now I
have to edit the translation and it takes hours. Hell of a job,
because I don't understand much of the stuff, not really.*

*My main concern is Granny's health because after the operation
her heart began to fail and she has developed bad headaches. I've
been living in the shadow of something horrible for too long. I've
started taking acupuncture treatment. The treatment and Judy's
philosophy take so much of my time that I can hardly breathe.*

Our dear Adolf is a father now. His wife has given birth to a baby girl. He is so busy that for two weeks he hasn't even studied English. With the shortages that exist it's absolutely impossible to acquire anything. The shops have been windswept. The existing commercial shops offer everything a baby may need. And the prices are out of this world. Boots – 700 rubles, a pair of shoes 500 rubles or more, a pair of panties – 35 rubles (the ones that you can restock in a basement of K-mart for 75 cents). Fabric shops offer Latvian applied art objects such as leather writing pads on ceramic, knick-knacks for out of the world prices. This is called "Transitional Economy."

I don't know what I am going to do about my job the next academic year. One idea is to work for a company full time and give lectures on Britain at the University. If only I knew what to do. The worst thing is that my optimism is failing me. I am getting more and more pessimistic.

Well, enough of this. Thank you for your hospitality. Be well, I hope to hear from you soon.

Love, Anita.

December 28, 1991

Dear Irene,

Thank you so much for the wonderful Christmas gifts! I finally got the parcel that you mailed on May 20. It arrived as a Christmas blessing, perfectly intact and not even bruised. Incredible! The Chinese bag is fantastic. The books are very interesting, so are the rest of the things.

The Latvian Republic got its independence at last, thank God! And it obviously doesn't know how to proceed. Prices are skyrocketing. A loaf of white bread that cost 18 kopecks at the beginning of the summer now costs five and a half rubles. There are enormous shortages of all types of goods. But we still endure. Even this way it is better than being a part of the Soviet Union.

I've changed my job. I've left the Faculty of Foreign Languages. Now I shall have only a few lectures there in Background Studies. I have changed for the Faculty of Theology, which is also part of the University of Latvia. Teaching English there is my part-time job. I am very satisfied with this change. What I gain is benevolence, peace and order, which is very important for my nerves. A business mafia rules the Foreign Language Faculty. They earn big money from pay groups, pay courses and the whole faculty modusoperandi falls into two groups, friends and non-friends. The students are OK of course, but I couldn't stand the atmosphere. At my new Faculty there are also some fringe benefits, like no night classes, a bit smaller workload, a bit bigger pay, free lunch for all, students and teachers paid by a church in Germany and better working conditions. I can have things duplicated for students.

(The rest of the letter has been lost.)

December 17, 1994

Riga

Judy and Janis got married. The wedding took place on August 20. Everything went off very smoothly. The ceremony was in St. Jacob's cathedral and followed by a small reception in a local restaurant. Janis and Judy study, want to get their master's degree in philosophy, hopefully this spring. They both work. Janis works at a medical school where he earns very little by teaching philosophy (all teachers and medical staff are below the official poverty level in Latvia today. The teachers even went on strike for a week and got a promise of a 16% raise somewhere in 1995.) Judy works as a secretary in an American company, hard

*work, but she earns enough to manage. She has also covered a
good part of her wedding expenses. I work at the School of
Theology (full-time) and at the School of Foreign Languages
(part-time) and in scores of other places translating and teaching
private classes. I can manage quite well, only the day is too short
and I have no free time or any days off.*

*My biggest problem today is that Granny got worse in the spring
and I have had to get up at night. A day before the wedding she
got better and we even took her to church but then she got worse
again. I realized that she's got Alzheimer's. Here nobody knows
what it means, but I do. My life has become almost unbearable.
My only hope is to survive a day and then to survive a night,
what with the workload and all. She has got short-term memory
loss; as a rule she doesn't recognize me and she wants to leave the
apartment all the time. Judy lives at Janis' place, so I have to
manage by myself. Even when she comes over she doesn't lift a
finger to help me. Janis has been a godsend. We have arranged
our timetables so that he stays here while I am at the University.
When I come home he's done everything: the floors have been
washed and Granny has been taken good care of. He is a warm
outgoing person. I get on with him very well. Without him I
would be practically dead. I mean deader than now. I've got all
kinds of ailments of nervous origin that I've been fighting off for
a long time. Granny managed to escape from the apartment on
Christmas and I spent three hours looking for her on the nearby
streets. Luckily we found her. Only as a result I've got a sharp
pain in the heart, some of the heart nerves are on strike. Janis
has got the hot hands of a healer. He has warmed my poor ribs
and I feel a little bit better. He doesn't know what to do with this
gift of God. He has automatically tranquilized Judy, of course. I
don't remember if I told you that I've got a specialist in
naturopathy, a doctor of holistic sciences who has helped me a lot.
He has found some homeopathic drugs that keep Granny in bed
for four hours. That means that I have to get up only once a
night, which is a blessing. I make some herbal tea and give it to
granny and survive the night. I wonder what medicine*

Alzheimer patients take in America for the night. You know that we have no hospitals or nursing homes for the patients of this kind. Someone must be with her all the time. I even found some woman who can stay with her when I am away but it costs some money. Riga is an expensive city now. It beats London and Copenhagen.

But enough is enough. I hope you haven't gotten depressed by my sorrowful wailing. I should count my blessings. I'm still managing. Janis has been of great moral support for me.

I am happy that you are doing well. I wonder when you are going to come over to Latvia. Don't worry you are not going to starve. Life is not easy but remembers that Latvians always enjoyed a good grumble and remember that you are always welcome. We'll try to be as good hosts as possible. Judy and Janis hosted two couples from the US, a week each in 1994 and they got a chance to go to Bristol for a week as part of a Friendship force venture. They returned only a week ago and they thoroughly enjoyed it. We had to pay part of the way and are still in debt, but then that was supposed to be their honeymoon. Janis fell in love with England. I do hope that I'll be able to embrace you on the Latvian soil one day.

I am sending you my best wishes to both of you. Enjoy the year of 1995, enjoy life and love.

Love, Anita.

ULDIS

In 1982, three years after I left Latvia, I received a surprise phone call and a subsequent letter from one of my English college professors by the name of Uldis. He was being sent by the Latvian State University to the USA in order to take an English Language course. In Riga I used to take private English lessons from Uldis in the course of which we became good friends. We would often vent our frustrations to each other. I remember how he complained to me about the fact that at the faculty meetings they always pestered the University professors about raising the level of their students' academic achievements. "When they start speaking about raising the level of our students' academic achievements," he said to me, "I feel as if I were standing up to my neck in the Baltic Sea spitting into the water, but its level just wouldn't rise."

I was surprised to hear that in five years after my departure from the Soviet Union, the country I left has changed so dramatically that University professors were allowed to travel abroad. The closest I had ever come to traveling out of Soviet Latvia was when I was teaching English at the Daugavpils Pedagogical College. I guess the bug of Perestroika was already in the air, for they sent a memo to our chairperson asking her to suggest a candidate for the trip to Great Britain for the purpose of professional development. This was something unheard of. The furthest we ever got to travel was the Moscow library and even that was considered a blessing. After much excitement and consideration a candidate was chosen and presented to the committee. It was one of our English teachers by the name of Lera. However, her candidacy was rejected. "It's because she is thirty-six years old," our chairperson explained to us apologetically. "You see, they don't send people over thirty five abroad, for heaven knows how many more years are left for them to live. What if they die at the age of forty? Just think of all the money that has been spent on them for nothing." Then either out of her naiveté or out of desperation, she selected me as the next possible candidate. Well, my candidacy was declined as well, the reasoning this time being that I had just started working on my thesis which might take me years to complete. Of course, no teacher was allowed to travel to London without completing her thesis.

In the meantime, the rumors went around that I had been chosen to go to Great Britain. As soon as I entered the office the teachers surrounded me asking,

-Irina, is it true that you are going to London?

-No, I am not.

-Why not? You are only twenty-six, aren't you?

-That's true, but I'm too tall.

-What?!

-You see, one of the requirements is that the person should be no taller than 5'8" and I am 6', neither do I fit into their weight requirements.

My colleagues stood there for some time studying my face for signs of laughter. There being none, they shrugged their shoulders and left. Truth, as you know, can be stranger than fiction.

The fact that my teacher Uldis was allowed to travel to the USA just seven years after this occurrence was significant and spoke of many changes that were yet to come.

Here is an extract from Uldis's letter.

"I saw your Mom, Dad and sister on June 13 before leaving for Arizona to attend summer English language courses. On August 4 we're returning to Tucson, on August 11 we're setting out home. So what might be called a life experience turns out to be only 50% so. Write to me to the given address and if you've got a phone, write your telephone number. By no means call me at my dorm because we're little children now. As far as children are concerned, mine are doing fine. Do you have any of your own? Write about yourself. Are you doing a thesis on Children's Literature?

Your folks are doing fine. Your Dad is put medically through his paces and doesn't think he'll be allowed to continue in his job. Your mom looks and acts just the same, the Tower of Strength of your family, a Rock of Ages. And as to Natalie, she has turned into your very image, so it's easier for me and don't please be jealous…"

"By no means call me at my dorm because we are all children now." *Uldis warns me not to* call him because the group of teachers from the Soviet Union is obviously under heavy KGB surveillance.

EDUCATION IN AMERICA

A symbol of our foreign language faculty was a parrot sitting on a dictionary which symbolized our process of learning these languages from those who themselves have learned them from a dictionary without ever speaking with foreigners, which by the way was strictly forbidden. As far as American education is concerned I view it as learning more and more about less and less and less about more and more which means that the students absorb as much knowledge about a chosen subject as possible but receive no information about anything else in life, such as literature, geography,music,theater or painting. Once I listened to an interview with a well known British actress. She said she was born in a poor family. "But make no mistake, we still went to the theater, we just didn't sit in the front row." I was exposed to the type of education where children are encouraged to explore any interest they have, provided it is not destructive, until they choose their own road in life. Without this, life in our modern society is difficult for children. Families fall apart, friends are rare. I have met very few people in whose life religion takes any significant place. In our lives there always comes the time when any interest outside ones profession will be helpful. This includes the end of our lives. Statistics show that people die five years after they retire. Yogis say that Americans are dead at fifty and buried at seventy.

In my time school played an important role. We were taught how to make soup and how to sow an apron. In times of Peter the Great the future tsars were taught how to mend their own socks and build ships. Nowadays schoolchildren leave schools without this knowledge. A famous British cook wrote that children in America don't know what vegetables look like. I thought that was a gross exaggeration until I attempted to buy veggies for dinner and the line of impatient customers had to help a checker to identify a beet.

I had a chance to observe children in a summer camp in Greenport. They are being taught how to walk as models on a runway. "Raise your knees higher, young ladies, higher their counselor keeps repeating. Many of these children are from poor families who even before they finish high school will have illegitimate children and end up on welfare. Wouldn't it make. more sense to teach them how to make a plate of soup or to sew an apron?

About ninety years ago my father, a chief marine engineer, went to France to accept a new ship in Paris. It was a humongous ship which at night looked like a city. My dad told us that the French were amazed at how quickly the Russian sailors learned to operate the vessel. They had no idea as to how long they had spent studying in school prior to that moment. They had spent eleven years in high school followed by four years at a special school for seamen.

I'm mostly surprised by the uniform thinking of American children. In the winter I taught English in a rural country school to a little Ecuadorian boy by the name of William. William was seven years old and was the only student in a class of fourteen that did not read English. That's why I was hired as an English as a Second Language teacher to work with him. I loved that little boy. He had a sturdy little body and a big head with beautiful intelligent dark brown eyes. His round face was the color of a smooth peach and his glistening dark hair was so thick it reminded me of fur. He looked different from American children, an obvious result of a different diet and life style. Many American children are either too thin and look like sprouts or are overweight. Some older girls in school loved hugging William. It probably felt like hugging a warm smooth pillow. William did not like being hugged and always tried to escape his much too loving female school mates.

As I come into the classroom, I hear his teacher Martha's voice. "And now children we will have math." Upon seeing me, William runs to my side and takes my hand. "Irina," he whispers to me, "They are going to have math and I'm going to have you." We settle down to the table in an empty dining hall. Today we are reading Hans Christian's fairy tale "The Real Princess." "There was once a prince who wished to marry a princess; but then she must be a real princess. He traveled all over the world in hopes of finding such a one, but there was always something wrong. Princesses he found plenty, but he couldn't make up his mind that they were real princesses, for one thing, or another, seemed to him not quite right about them." Here, William stops and raises at me his big serious eyes, "Irina, why have you brought me such a sad story? I almost feel like crying."

On Friday I come to school a little early. Children are at recess. William is hanging over the rail of the banister. "How is my William today?" I ask him lightly patting him on his back. "Good" he says breathing heavily. "Irina, I hear his teacher's concerned voice calling me from the top of the steps. I turn around. "You shouldn't pat William on his back, she warns me lowering her voice, "You might be accused of touching his private parts."

Ann is a ninety two year old teacher who likes to stop by our yard and reminisce about her teaching days in a middle school. Once she told me about a difficult student she had in her class. His name was Mike. He became such a pest that she threatened to punish him if he continued bothering his classmates. "If you don't stop it I am going," she stopped for a moment trying to think of some horrible punishment," I am going to kiss you." "Oh no, Miss Ann!," Mike exclaimed. He behaved himself for a long time, but when he brought his dog to school, Miss Ann ordered the class to catch the perpetrator and hold him. They enjoyed doing it. Miss Ann kissed Mike on his left cheek. Afterwards Mike never misbehaved again.

When I heard this story I asked Ann if she knows what would happen to her if she did it now. "I would lose my job." she said.

Later I observed the following scene. William has just come back after spending two months with his grandparents in Ecuador. Upon seeing him in the corridor, Helen, the school counselor welcomes him back and asks him for permission to give him a hug. Without much enthusiasm William expresses his consent and having shyly averted his face, offers her his lifeless body. He looks as if he were about to swallow a dose of a much disliked medicine. Helen gives him a hug after which he gives a sigh of relief and runs away. I have often found the lack of touching in America between couples, parents and children, teachers and high school children, professors and their students rather puzzling. Both sides are missing out a lot. Doctors say that touching activates the immune system.

It reminds me of a joke. They were observing couples from different countries, trying to establish how often they touched each other while sitting and talking in a cafe. Russians touched each other fifteen times an hour, Italians thirteen times, French twelve times, and as far as the English are concerned observers are still waiting for that to happen.

When I was being accessed by our dean for the position of Assistant Professor at our college, the main objection for me to get that position was that I was in the habit of putting my hand on the shoulder of a student who has called me asking for help with his work. I was so used to doing it that I found it difficult to comply. In spite of this I did get the title of Assistant Professor.

Once I got a call from school. A teacher became sick and they were looking for a substitute. "Could you come and help us?" I came. The students had an assignment. They had to write a letter to their pen pals in Great Britain. It was a very disciplined group of students. They came into the computer room and took their places at the tables. Each of them had their own computer. When they started working I looked at what they were writing. The assignment was "write about your day." They all came from school at the same time and had dinner. Their favorite dinner was meatballs and spaghetti in tomato sauce. They all watched TV and then did their homework. It sounded as if their assignments were written by the same hand. Someone said about young Americans, "The more they try to be different from each other the more they are the same."

It makes me think of an experiment once conducted in the Soviet Union. A group of ten journalists were given the beginning lines of the same article and asked to complete it. This resulted in ten almost identical articles. In the Soviet Union it could be explained by the restriction of the Soviet regime. Why though is the same thing happening in America, the land of the free, to American children? An American writer once asked a Russian writer why in the land of Tolstoy and Dostoevsky that there was such a proliferation of bad literature. The Russian writer explained that Soviet censorship eliminated all the significant stuff. "And now let me ask you what your excuse is for having such a vast number of bad books on the market?," he asked his American counterpart.

The greatest difference between our two societies is that in America there is no intelligentsia. In Europe it is always the intelligentsia that shows the new direction of a country. Here in America it is shown by beautiful people in Hollywood. Smart people here don't coalesce in a class and they remain apart. At the college where I was teaching, a literary magazine was published with students' and teachers' writings. I submitted to the magazine the first chapter of my book of memoirs. It described how I was leaving Latvia in 1979. The magazine accepted the article. My students who read it said that they greatly appreciated it. On the other hand, the teachers never said a word even though from their reaction and glances toward me I could clearly see that they had read the chapter. In Latvia after reading such an account members of the faculty would invariably initiate a lot of discussion from what one of their colleagues had written. In the U.S. such exchange of opinions on the part of my colleagues did not even exist. A new book, play or concert is never discussed in the adjunct room. Here teachers speak about their students, mortgages, illnesses and family situations. It is a different world I say to myself.

In the U.S. people like Woody Allan, Steve Jobs, Bill Gates and Mark Zukersberg all reached much success without an extensive formal education. This phenomenon has given an idea to much of the younger generation that they could also reach success without having much education. In the Soviet Union education was valued as a necessity in becoming a well rounded individual. Having a pretty face or great wealth is not enough. To inspire young people they have to be touched by wisdom. For one to convey wisdom one has to have been exposed to a variety of life experiences and to have explored a variety of interests. The more multisided an individual has become the more wisdom they will obtain. This multisidedness is lacking here in schools as teachers have become more like monosided educators. Perhaps this monosideness on the part of these educators has contributed to the marked increase of suicide among the adolescent population in this country. A young generation in any culture requires answers to their questions, concerns and problems. Where parents fail to give answers

AIDS BENEFIT

It was the women who caught my attention first. Obese and amorphous, they were slowly walking down the street like bovine animals on their way to the watering hole. To my eye they appeared to be somewhat unfinished. I imagined that a sculptor who was making clay figurines, had thrown together big lumps of clay, and after molding their heads was called to attend to some urgent matter. The lumps got bored of waiting, got up and walked out of the house. Now they are out there, huge and amorphous roaming the world in pants and T-shirts and there is no bringing them back. I followed the women and came to the building of a local "Y" with a big sign "AIDS BENEFIT" over the door.

In a steady stream men were coming to the "Y" as well. Contrary to the women, most of them were well molded. Tall, with shapely legs and athletic torsos, they were also well groomed and dressed. Some wore mustache and others had nose or belly button rings. Women settled on the steps of the "Y", joking, laughing loudly and patting each other on the back. In spite of their primeval size they were lighthearted and playful, perhaps too playful for the occasion. Men, who found their presence alarming, kept watching them out of the corner of the eye. Most of the men went in right away and after a while walked out briskly. Breathing deeply like divers under the water they could stay in the building for a short time only. The intensity of their emotions, their somber tragic faces clashed with their playful appearance, tanned shapely legs, athletic torsos, earrings, bracelets, exotic hairdos and exquisite clothes. After a while they would return to the "Y".

Some people would come out of the "Y" in tears and immediately start talking or laughing loudly.

There were some striking couples. There was a young man with a pair of the most beautiful shapely legs that I have ever seen. He wore a pair of brightly colored shorts and held on a leash a tiny white dog whose fur was tied in many multi-colored bows. He was chaperoned by an older dignified gray-haired gentleman.

Two tall almost identical blondes, still beautiful in their early forties, coiffured, perfumed, and tastefully dressed, came out, sat down on a bench in front of the "Y," talking, laughing animatedly, and then simultaneously burst into tears.

There were some heterosexual couples with small children. An old couple shuffled slowly towards the "Y", fanning themselves with newspapers.

A big family was being photographed against a quilt. "To my cousin, my nephew, my son, who died at 32 years of age," read the inscription on the quilt.

A strikingly beautiful young black lady with a pair of long legs, which seemed even longer on account of high-heeled elegant shoes, emerged from the "Y" sobbing.

A blonde, a black man. A mother and a daughter. Who are they grieving for?

Some people have lost a loved one only recently and their loss was like a gaping bottomless wound. For others the loss was further removed in time and the pain was like a pricking thorn.

This disease has changed us all. There is not a person who hasn't been robbed by it. It is in our midst. It is here to stay. AIDS is breathing down our neck and waiting for the next human sacrifice. Nobody is exempt. Nobody is safe. Nobody.

Every culture cultivates its particular form of insanity. In my country schizophrenia was the prevalent mental disorder. The fact that we were constantly watched by the Big Brother, the fear of KGB, the existence of Gulag fostered this particular form of insanity.

In this country I observe that many people are suffering from obsessive-compulsive disorder, which may be due to the fact that relaxation has not been programmed into American life the way it is in other countries. The Carnival in Brazil is one such example. During the year many impressionable minds are preoccupied with preparations for the Carnival. Special suits are ordered, dances are practiced, songs are learned. Money is earned for the expensive carnival outfits. Then the Carnival comes. People are off from work for weeks. They sing, dance on the streets or sprawl themselves on the beach. This gives Brazilians a glimpse of a different reality, different sounds, colors and smells.

In the Soviet Union relaxation and socializing were programmed into people's daily lives as well. Since work was a right in my old country, everybody worked, which translated into everybody doing little work for little money. There was a saying. "They pretend that they pay us and we pretend that we work."

I remember a joke about a supervisor who comes into his boss' office with a puzzled look on his face "Comrade Ivanov," he reports, "I am at a loss as to what to do with our work force. After yesterday's national holiday all our workers are sleeping at their desks. I've just checked again. It's lunchtime but everybody is still asleep. To which the wise boss responds, "Well, in this case, let them work without lunch today."

With such work ethics, there was plenty of time for people to socialize, celebrate, get drunk and do all sorts of exciting things at work.

In America there is no programmed relaxation time. As a rule, vacation is no longer than two weeks a year and often even less than that. All national holidays are one day long. A National Health magazine reports that in 2003 American employees gave back to their companies twenty-one billion dollars in unused vacation time and that seventeen per cent of Americans take no vacation at all. Thus, Americans are constantly working or resting after work or are preparing for one. Hence, the terrible disease of obsessive-compulsive disorder has been programmed into this culture.

WAITING FOR A SIGN

Please look down as you are peddling along
on your unpolluted cloud.
I am sure there is one or two left around..
Please, look down at me.
Here I am in Brooklyn USA,
the third continent on your left,
on the sixth floor in a one bedroom apartment between 64 and 65 Street.
Look down
and let me feel your presence and your grace.
They say you've created us in your image.
There are so many images around.
Which one is yours?
They say you've created us.
Was it fun?
You've got to follow up on your creation.
Well, do you know what's happening to us?
Please look down and let me feel you know.
You've made this Earth and put a big orange sun in the sky.
Now both are ailing.
It's getting very hot down here.
Are you gonna let us burn alive?
Show us your mercy, look down at us as you are passing by.
How are you feeling?
Did you get old or did you get insane?
Or did you just forget us?
We're still down here,
still waiting for a sign.
They say these are the last days.

It sure feels like it.
It's hard to breathe.
Before it all comes to an end
I want to know that you are watching
and you're well informed.
I want to know you hear me,
for here I am calling out to you
from Brooklyn, USA.
I've been created in your image
and I am waiting for a sign. So please look down.

LIVING IN NEW YORK

Before moving to Long Island, for a little over twenty years I lived in New York City where I taught English as a Second Language at the City University. Americans say that New York is not America because so many more immigrants than Americans live there. Living in New York gave me an opportunity to observe different groups of immigrants. In the land of the free, Asians became enamored with enormous TV sets, tape recorders, cameras and other complex machinery. Caribbeans were willing to sacrifice anything for a house of their own. Russians, who in their own country were denied access to the rest of the world, would become drunk on freedom and as soon as they got back on their feet, start traveling around the world. Americans watched them suspiciously wondering where they got the money to travel like this. Americans spent their money cautiously. Many of them have never traveled out of their country, and some have seldom ventured out of their city or even their neighborhood. They did not exhibit much interest in history, geography or foreign languages. An African ESL student of mine by the name of Bamba once told me that before settling down in America he traveled in Europe extensively and was eager to meet American blacks but never did. He was curious why there were no American blacks in Europe and was told that they were poor and had no money to travel. "But now I am here," he said to me,"and I know that they do have the money. For some reason, they just don't like to travel."I have not escaped the Russian stereotype and traveled hungrily and extensively since I left Latvia in 1979. On my way to America I've been to Austria and Italy. My first trip out of America was to Mexico in 1982. After that my future husband Bruce and I traveled to England, The Caribbean (St.Thomas and Barbados), Canada, Paradise Island, France, Israel, Cancun and Puerto Rico, Germany. Two years ago I went to Hungary. As I am writing this, I am planning to visit my cousin in Germany. Wherever I went, I would always send home to Latvia pictures and letters with detailed description of the places I had visited. I have saved some of the letters. Here is one of them.

Dear Dimkovichs,

Two days ago we returned from Barbados where we spent ten days swimming in the Atlantic Ocean regardless of the fact that I was sick with the flu, which I got in NY a day before our departure. Barbados is a small island with a pirate history. We've done a lot of swimming here. We have also visited the Botanical Gardens where we have seen many exotic plants, tasted a Passion fruit and a Golden apple, had our pictures taken with an incredible orange and blue flower called 'A Bird of Paradise' in the background and drank a delicious drink made of milk, peanut butter, honey and a bitter spice called Angosta. We have seen a local show and went to a stalactite cave that looked like a moon crater. The island is populated by the black people with a proud, straight, royal posture. I think they have developed this posture because it is impossible to die from hunger or cold in Barbados. The island is full of coconut trees and it is so hot that you can sleep right on the beach. There is nowhere to rush. The last ship had departed and nobody gave its departure any attention.

Bruce loves to stand on his head in the water, revealing to the world his long shapely legs. He demonstrated this art on the beach. Next day half of the local population was standing on their heads in the water. However, they were doing it creatively. They were either spreading their legs widely in a letter 'V' or, while still in the letter 'V' position, bending one leg and touching the knee of the other leg and holding this position for quite some time.

After three years of intensive training on NY beaches and Bruce's quite justified indignation at my inability to throw a Frisbee straight, I have finally learned the art. We demonstrated our newly acquired ability on the beach in Barbados. All eyes being on us, I tried to do my best. Next day the local guys were playing Frisbee on the beach and their version was a far cry from ours. They used every part of their beautiful flexible free bodies. One of the players would throw the Frisbee up in the air. It would travel for about 25 meters, touch the ground, bounce off, rise in the air again and then fly another 25 meters. After this it would stop over the head of the other player as if hypnotized and spin patiently, waiting to be caught. Upon seeing the approaching Frisbee, the recipient would jump high up in the air, perform a somersault and then on the way back to the Earth grab the revolving Frisbee. Should he have missed the plate, he would throw himself on the ground, growling, moaning and displaying his total remorse. This sight has rid me of any desire to compete.

Now we are back in NY. This year is going to be rather difficult for me. I will be teaching 24 hours at the Technical College and 6 hours at Kingsboro. It happened because I didn't know if they would give me hours in the latter. I have no idea of how I am I going to juggle all these hours, but I'll survive.

Love, Irina.

MY SISTER NATALIE

When my parents first moved to Riga they owned a pair of handsome German shepherds. Once I was born, taking care of a baby and two pets in a city became too much for my mom and the dogs had to be given away. Seven years later my sister Natalie was born. While very young we had our share of fights. I remember dad saying, "Look at this. I used to own a pair of beautiful dogs. Now I have a pair of big fat fools who are always fighting and screaming. Why on earth did I need this?" And he would roll his eyes up as if awaiting for the answer from above. No answer ever came. By the age of twenty Natalie and I had outgrown our cat fights and became friends. However, a year before my departure from Latvia my sister stopped talking to me. I did not know what had caused her to behave in such a way and many times asked her why she would not talk to me but she gave me no explanation and remained locked in her silence. I tried to tell her about my decision to emigrate but each time I entered her room; she would turn her back to me. Being unable to break the news of such magnitude to her unyielding back I would retreat in silence. Finally it was my parents who told her the news. Emigrating in those times was as close as one could get to dying. It meant that we would never see each other again. But even that didn't melt my sister's cold silence. On the eve of my departure Natalie went to the theater and having come home late at night described the merits of the performance to my friends who came to say their good byes to me. They listened to her intellectual talk in sadness.

Once I reached New York I wrote letters home addressing them collectively to our cat Dimka, for it was too dangerous to address them to any one person in particular. It was common knowledge that the

KGB closely monitored all communications that came from abroad. Instead of sending my letters home I used to send them to my aunt and uncle who lived in Klaipeda (Lithuania). They were already retired at the time and thus out of danger. My parents corresponded with me. Natalie never wrote a line. Then our cat, Dimka, died. After that our mother passed away. Then came Chernobyl. I think around that time I received her first letter. It was short. She wrote that she was expecting a child. In October, 1986 she gave birth to a baby girl and called her Anna Maria. I sent her baby bottles, blankets and toys. After the birth of Anna Maria my sister sounded upbeat and more together. She sent me some pictures of the baby. My niece didn't look like anyone on our side of the family. When Latvia ceased to be a part of the Soviet Union the situation there grew increasingly unstable. Natalie asked me to send them a letter of invitation so that they too, could emigrate. Even though I did send the invitation to them right away, it had to make its way through Washington; the whole process was taking too much time. Feeling that they had to emigrate as soon as possible, Natalie made a decision to go to Israel instead. Shortly after reaching Israel she stopped writing. Again there was no explanation. I honored her silence. When my niece was about to turn seven I sent her a birthday card and a tape with children's songs. She answered with a letter. That's when I decided that it was time to introduce myself to her and thus comply with the wish that my dad had expressed in one of his last letters. "It's time for you to meet your niece," he wrote in it, "She needs you." He wrote in it. I invited Bruce to join me and he agreed. Not knowing how Natalie would take my coming over, I didn't let her know that I was on my way. To make sure that they would be home at the time of our arrival I called her and told her that Bruce was about to visit Israel on business and would deliver a birthday present to my niece. I asked her what the best birthday present for Anna would be and she answered,"A box of watercolors." I also asked her if there was a hotel in town where Bruce could stay for a night, and she invited him to stay with them in their apartment.

All I knew about her at the time was that she was living in Arad, a small town near the Dead Sea, where she taught English to high school students who had nicknamed her Gorilla and often jumped out of the windows of the second floor classroom during her class. I also knew that Anna was now called Anat. The change of the name came because the name Anna rhymed with 'banana' and that was what the school kids called her, "Anna-banana." She hated being teased and changed her name to Anat. I bought a big box of watercolors in an Art supply store in Manhattan, and we ordered tickets to Tel Aviv.

Upon our arrival in Israel Bruce called Natalie from our hotel and they set up the time for a meeting. Natalie and Anat would meet him the next day at a bus stop in Arad.

On the way to Arad I was surprised by the intensity of my emotions. I was glad that it was dark on the bus. In Israel they turn the lights off on buses at night in order to prevent them from becoming a target for terrorists. I did not have to hide my face. I had not seen my sister in sixteen years. I remembered a slim pale girl with bushy hair and melancholy eyes. I remembered how she came to see me off at the railway station in Riga. In silence she took two tiny silver rings off her finger and put them on mine. She didn't say a word, nor did she cry.

When we arrived in Arad, the lights on the bus went on and the doors opened. I heard somebody calling out Bruce's name. I opened my eyes and saw a big woman with Natalie's head standing in front of the bus. I bent down so that she couldn't see me... "It's Natalie." I whispered to him. Bruce got up and walked towards the front door. I exited through the back door with other passengers and sank into the dark Israeli night. It felt like being on the bottom of a deep well. In this darkness I followed Bruce's white shirt for quite some time until I realized that I was following the wrong man. I found myself lost in the middle of the night on the outskirts of a small town in a country whose language I didn't speak. Of a few people who ventured outside at that late hour, no one seemed to be too eager to help me. Finally, I saw an unmistakably stocky figure of a Russian woman and asked her in Russian how to get to the street that I was looking for. "Follow me,' she said and walked ahead briskly. After about five minutes she pointed to a six-story building. "This is the house you are looking for," she said. I turned around to thank her but she was gone having disappeared into the darkness as quickly and mysteriously as she had appeared before me.

The elevator being broken, I climbed to the top floor, rang the bell and pushed the door open. It was unlocked. A little girl with auburn hair was sitting on a sofa holding a doll in her arms. I waived to her and pressed my finger against my lips asking her to be silent which she did with her mouth open looking at me intently. At that moment my sister Natalie walked into the room. She looked at me in astonishment and asked if Bruce knew I was there. I answered that he did. "Well, this is some surprise!" she exclaimed and offered me to sit down and relax while she was making tea in the kitchen.

I sat down on the sofa. It was hot and stuffy even though the window was wide open. I looked around. They lived in a two-bedroom apartment with a balcony, a TV-set and a neurotic cat that kept jumping all around the living room. I could hear a washer working in the kitchen. It surprised me that the room bore no sign of Natalie's personality or any trace of her quite significant artistic talent. The apartment was bare of spirit and reminded of an illustration of an apartment in an English textbook. "There is a window in the living room. A sofa is to the left of the window. A TV set is in front of the sofa."

My niece was a funny kid with bushy hair, red cheeks and very pale skin. She was smart, spoiled and playful. When we took her out the next day, she asked me to buy her a pirogue. We went into a bakery immersed in the sweet warm smell of baked bread and pastry. "This is my aunt from America," she announced proudly to the man behind the counter. The baker nodded seriously but there was a smile behind his somber front. He gave her a potato pirogue that immediately disappeared in her mouth. An exchange in Hebrew followed out of which I understood two words "America" and "New York". Later Anat showed us around Arad. It was a small quiet town where she knew every dog and cat by name. She petted every one of them and they returned her affection by licking her hands and face.

That night the four of us went to the new shopping mall which was the town's main attraction. At the mall Anat requested a hamburger. After getting her one we sat down at a table and Bruce went to get us Cokes. That's when Anat sank her teeth into the burger, turned to her mom and said calmly but decisively, "Go home." Natalie turned to her in disbelief. "Go home," the child repeated, "I want to be with my aunt." Natalie's face flooded with embarrassment. I was struggling to find the right words but each time the pain I saw in my sister's face threw me off my feet as if it were a powerful ocean wave. I shrugged my shoulders apologetically. I watched her step on the escalator. She moved as if pierced by a spear. The child continued calmly chewing her hamburger and making circles in the puddle of ketchup with her potato chips. Bruce appeared at the table with two cokes and asked where Natalie was. "She's left. Please go and catch up with her." I said. He felt the urgency in my voice, got up, and got on the escalator. Later he told me that when he left the mall he saw Natalie walking in the dark, moving slowly and with difficulty as if pierced by a dagger. He hoped that he had made a mistake and it wasn't her but when he came closer there was no denying that it was my sister. She turned to him. "So she sent you away as well?" He nodded.

When we with Anat finally returned home from the mall, Bruce, Natalie and I sat down in the kitchen to share a bottle of wine. As Natalie was getting tipsy a dark cloud of wrath descended upon her. "Why has she taken to you? Why you? Why you?" She kept repeating obsessively. Paralyzed by her anger I didn't know what to say. It was clear that all was lost and we would never be sisters again. Finally I told her that it was late and we had to go to bed. "We should get out early tomorrow," I whispered to Bruce when we were alone in the room. He nodded in the dark. I lay beside him for a long time unable to fall asleep. On the other side of the wall there was my niece so surprisingly familiar to me in all her thoughts, reactions and gestures, so innocently in love with me, her aunt.

Early next morning we left the house without saying good-bye. In the evening I called to apologize. Anat picked up the phone. "It was too early, honey. You were sleeping. We didn't want to wake you up." I tried to explain to her. "I understand." The child said with the sadness and finality that brought tears to my eyes. Natalie took the receiver. "Your niece has been overcome by grief," she said. We decided to meet in Tel Aviv before our departure from Israel.

When I hung up the phone I cried because I felt that even though all was lost between me and my sister, I did not undertake this trip in vain, for my niece and I loved each other. I cried because for the first time I fully realized the immense dislike my sister held for me and how relentless it was. She was crippled by it the way trees growing on the shore get crippled by the strong ocean wind. I cried because of our inability to talk to each other and because there was no hope left for us. I felt like I had traveled around half the globe to get to the charmed castle only to realize that the key to it was lost forever. I cried about my far away native country Latvia that I had not seen in sixteen long years, about my unhappy family, about my parents who died without uttering a word of kindness and about us the two offspring of my parents' unhappiness who were unable to find words for each other. And with those tears the wound that had festered for almost two decades finally began to heal.

When I met them in Tel Aviv four days later I was a different person and they didn't know me. I met them calmly, with a smile, and without any feeling of attachment because on the night we spent in the kitchen together, my sister and I had died to each other. Whatever illusions either of us had entertained about bridging the gap between us upon our reunion were gone and with their departure came a certain feeling of lightness. I felt as if for years I had been carrying a heavy suitcase only to realize that the clothes in it had been eaten by moths or were hopelessly out of fashion. That's when I left the suitcase on the corner and felt instant relief. As far as my niece Anat was concerned, the time was too short, the distance too long and the hatred in her mother's heart too strong for any meaningful relationship to develop and that's where we left off at that time.

Natalie, 4 years old with Irina, 11 years old

Irina, 13 with Natalie, 6, and their grandfather

FOND MEMORIES OF MY CHILDHOOD

Saulkrasti

Far away on the other side of the globe there is a country called Latvia. About fifty kilometers from its capital Riga, on the shore of the Baltic Sea lies a village called Saulkrasti which translates into English as "The Sunny Shores." Latvia has a temperate climate and it rains a lot in that part of the world. For some reason Saulkrasti differs in this respect from the rest of the country for it seldom rains in "The Sunny Shores." As a child I spent summers there. In those days in Latvia children used to spend summer months away from home. Their parents would either send them to their relatives who lived in the country, rent a cottage or else pay for their children's stay in a summer camp in the country.

Our family rented a place in Saulkrasti, which in those days used to maintain itself as a fishing village. In the afternoon we would watch fishermen return home from the sea, get out of their old sturdy boats and spread the fish nets out in the sun to dry. There our mom would often buy the most delicious smoked eels and we would eat them right on the beach with our hands, sitting on the sand smooth and tender like baby's skin and afterwards wash our hands in cold salty water.

Between the sea and the road stands a big hill on top of which our landlord Peter Onculs built a wooden bench for the people to rest on after a long climb in the hot silky sand. At the bottom of the hill lies a valley where the sun happily plays with the wind lighting up bright sunny patches each time the strong sea wind moves the branches of the tall pine trees. The bottom of the valley is covered with ferns and the short grass called "Bunny's ear", which we children liked to chew on. It has a mild sour taste. There also grow tiny white flowers that breathe sweet smell into the air. It is quiet here because people don't go down onto this valley. They avoid it because they like to take a short cut. They are either hot and eager to get to the beach, or hungry and tired from sunbathing and swimming and are in a hurry to get home. So it is all mine. It has opened me up with its every fern, leaf and flower. I sit here for a long time taking in the smells, the shadows, the happy interplay of the sun and the wind. I listen to the silence. Here God speaks to me and I understand Him.

The valley is holding me in its palms and I feel protected. It is there untouched in my memory and nothing can change it, even if a spa has been built on top of that hill or if it is true that the Baltic Sea has gotten so polluted that people no longer swim in it. I am still there and it is mine to keep. The suntanned girl in a red dress, the valley full of white flowers and ferns and the sound of the waves are suspended in time. I hear the strong call of the Baltic Sea. I feel its powerful breath on my face.

Having finally reached the top of the hill, I stop, breathe in the cool salty air and admire the white foam of the waves on the deep aquamarine of the sea. My ankles sink deep into the hot sand as I run down the hill to greet the sea, to honor it, to touch it. I especially love doing this in the spring, since Latvian winters last seven long rainy months. When the first rays of the spring sun hit the earth I run down the hill, sprawl myself on the shore like a shipwrecked sailor and put my hands into the cold salty water. It is so cold, it makes my hands ache.

Oh, Baltic Sea, when the summer finally comes and you take me in your arms, when you lull me, when you hum to me your endless song, my wounds heal. I love being beside you at night. I can't see you, but I feel your breath on my face and sense your magnificent presence. I can hear you rolling, tossing and sighing in your enormous bed like a big, dark and powerful beast. Your sighs, your waves, the moonlight dancing on your endless being…

In the daytime you are as innocent and playful as a young animal. I walk for miles along the shore among the seashells, jelly fish, pieces of fish nets and smooth stones that you have generously sprawled under my feet. I bring home your scent and your gifts, delicate pink shells, dead crabs, colorful stones and bits and pieces of precious golden amber. Writing this is my way of getting back with you, even though we are so far apart. I am writing this to you, the Baltic Sea, from America, New York.

DIMKA

Like every child I was always pestering my parents about getting a dog, a cat or a sister and always in the same order. I never got the first wish but a cat and a sister were granted to me. I got a cat the day my grandpa's friend came over and brought me a blue box. When I opened it–a ball of grey fur rolled out and hid under a wardrobe. The next morning a beautiful kitten emerged and ran straight to the saucer full of milk from which he drank hungrily. I tiptoed closer and admired his fur and a quick pink tongue. He was not a European cat like all my friends had, but a Siberian one, with unusual long fur and thus much bigger in size. Because of his grey-bluish coat we named him Dinka, which is a tender word for fog in Russian. Dimka grew up to be so huge that when he would come out to meet our first time visitors, they would freeze in awe and refuse to move beyond the threshold. He was so handsome that his portrait painted by a well-known Latvian artist Berzinya got stolen from a picture gallery where it was exhibited, while mine was left hanging on the wall, a fact for which I never forgave him.

In those days we would spend summers near the Baltic Sea and we would always bring Dimka with us. Being a city slicker he felt threatened by the trees, strong sea wind and tall grass. Jumping frogs and cacling hens made him nervous. At night local Tom cats chased him up a tall pine tree that grew near our summer cottage. Fear of local cats would catapult Dimka right to the top of the tree, but he had no idea how to get back down. In the morning when we would open the door of our cottage, we would be greeted by his loud doleful cries coming from the sky. We would raise out heads and there was Dimka bewailing his destiny on the top branch of a tall pine tree. This would gather a crowd of neighbors. Among them would be a big round tante Zaiga with her enormous bosom covered by an apron, her snotty son Uldis whose pants threatened to slide off his bottom, two sisters, Datse and Mara, whose long blond pigtails were the subject of my secret envy, and of course our gentle giant of a landlord, Peter oncul. His son Janis would bring a big straw basket. Peter oncul would then tie it to the end of a long rope and get the rope over the branch from which the unfortunate cat was loudly calling out for help. The basket would be pulled to the level of the branch and Dimka was firmly instructed to jump in. First he would sniff the basket suspiciously, then relieve himself on the crowd and finally gracefully jump into the basket which would then be lowered down to the accompaniment of the happy cheers of onlookers.

There was a significant flaw in his otherwise cuddly and friendly personality. Dimka hated loud noises. In fact he was on a crusade against them and was taking any source of such personally. One of his enemies happened to be my father's leather coat which he disliked with great passion. At night when my father would return home from work in the shipyard and take off his long brown leather coat, it would make a loud hostile rustling sound. Dimka would first back up into the corner of the corridor and hiss, trying to scare the coat into silence. Then, having failed to do so, he would gather all his feline strength and courage and attack the coat ferociously. This would annoy my father to no end since he like Dimka had a big ego and took all attacks on his belongings personally.

When my second wish was given to me and my sister Natasha was born, she cried a lot. Dimka avoided coming near her. He would sit on the threshold of the room where her crib was, sniff at the air suspiciously and look into my eyes. How come, he seemed to be saying, that such a little animal causes so much noise and commotion. It just wasn't right. When Natasha started walking, she would often fall. Her high pitched wailing was beyond Dimka's tolerance level. The moment she would let out a scream the cat would assume a warrior position and charge at her. This would only intensify Natasha's screams and bring into the room my angry mom, who in turn would scream and wave a kitchen utensil at the hissing cat, trying to scare him away from the crying toddler. All this commotion, of course, would bring my grandfather out of his study with his glasses on his forehead and his moustache risen up questioningly which automatically was supposed to end any commotion in our house and bring peace into the world.

During one such episode our mom failed to appear in the room fast enough and Dimka scratched my sister. Thus the decision was made to part with the cat. Dimka went to live with my father's friend Anatole and his wife Anne. There he lived for many years well cared for by those kind people who loved him and respected his need for peace and tranquility. When we would come over for a visit, we would always bring Dimka his favorite delicacy, a piece of smoked fish. After devouring it he would spread his big heavy body in my lap and sing me a thank you song.

Now I live in the big city of New York without dogs, cats or sisters, but this memory keeps me warm. At times when I am feeling low I sit down and sing myself Dimka's thank you song and that never fails to make me feel better.

TUTTI

Tutti was another pet who lived with us in Riga. One warm spring afternoon my sister Natalie brought home a little baby bird that had fallen out of its nest in our backyard. It was fluffy with a big wide open beak that kept screaming for food. Since the rule set by our great patriarch, our grandpa, declared that there be no birds in the house. So it was that Tutti lived illegally in a shoe box hidden in the corner of the kitchen and was allowed to cross the kitchen borders only when our grandpa was out of the house. We fed it pink worms, white bread soaked in milk, and when it grew older, tiny strips of red meat. When Natalie had first brought it home we were not sure what kind of bird Tutti was, but it was growing fast, and soon grew out of the shoe box, first its beak and then the rest of it, taking the shape of a beautiful young black crow. I loved to hold it and feel the beat of its heart beneath my palms.

When Tutti started flying around the house we discovered that it was growing up to be a thief. Anything that sparkled had to be hidden from Tutti who otherwise would grab it and fly away with it. This included spoons and buttons, necklaces and rings, brooches and earrings. Sometimes we would find the missing object in Tutti's shoe box, other times we couldn't find it for weeks and my mother's golden earring disappeared forever. Tutti was allowed into every room with the exception of grandpa's study. My mother was determined to keep Tutti's presence in the house a secret from him. But one day the inevitable happened. Grandpa went out and left the door of the room open. Nobody saw Tutti fly in and settle on top of a tall bookshelf filled with medical books. When grandpa returned to his room and sat down at the table to read his medical journal, Tutti fascinated by the shiny glow of his bald head that was transformed into a golden globe by the bright light of a table lamp, landed right on top of it. It probably decided to investigate if it could steal that too. Grandpa got up and walked with Tutti adorning his head right into the kitchen and said indignantly to our mother who was at the stove cooking dinner: "Tonya, take this thing off my head, will you?" That's how the secret got out.

The day came when Tutti flew out of the window. From our window we saw it fly across the street through the open window of a second floor apartment. We ran into the building and rang the bell. A woman in an apron opened the door and smiled at us. She must have been cooking for delicious smells followed her and traveled into the staircase. "Excuse us, we pleaded with her, "but our crow Tutti is in your apartment." The woman patiently assured us that there were no crows in her apartment. "But we saw it fly through your open window!" exclaimed Natalie who was on the verge of tears. The woman led us into her living room and there was Tutti sitting on top of her secretary next to a huge vase with red tulips, looking at us mischievously.

When the summer came we brought Tutti with us to the seaside where our family used to rent a summer cottage and let it out into the world of sunshine, tall pines and blooming apple trees. At first Tutti was coming home at the end of each day to spend nights with us. Then it started checking in with us in the middle of the day. Tutti would sit on a branch of a blooming apple tree that grew in front of our cottage and call out to us. When we would run out to greet it, Tutti would gracefully land on the doorsteps and allow us to feed and pet it. By the end of July Tutti was coming home once a week and by the end of the summer Tutti was coming home no more. But it came to bid us goodbye when we were leaving for the city.

They say that crows live for a hundred years. I hope so. It warms my heart to think that somewhere in my old country Tutti is flying around in the pine forest near the Baltic Sea which I loved so much. It's like a part of me is still there flying around.

MY THOUGHTS, OBSERVATIONS AND PICTURES IN WORDS

Last night transit workers went on strike. When there is a strike in New York, people watch Union reps make speeches on TV. It is a different story in Italy. I remember when a bus to Rome suddenly stopped in the middle of nowhere; the driver got out, lay down on the grass and unwrapped his sandwich. After he had slowly eaten it and with a hardy appetite, he announced to his bewildered passengers who were watching him out of the windows that he was on strike until three o'clock and invited them to get off the bus and stretch their legs. In the meantime, the New York media is reporting that last night there were no homicides in New York. I seems that both potential victims and criminals are trying to figure out how to get back home.

Last Saturday Orthodox Jews were picketing Waldbaums, the only supermarket in the Jewish neighborhood of Boro Park that stays open on the Sabbath. They were demanding its closure on the Sabbath. There was a lot of screaming, shouting and excitement. An old insane Jewish woman in ragged clothes was making her way through the crowds. She must have mistaken the stars on police cars for the Star of David because she kissed each and every one of them and then happily waved a little Israeli flag to the skies.

Crystal vases and figurines are a status symbol in Russia. Our neighbor Tsvy, the owner of a store on Avenue U told me that he was amazed to see a line form in front of his store early in the morning. This was probably the only line he saw in America. The line consisted entirely of Russian emigrants. "They all bought crystal vases," he said in awe.

At the end of the ESL course that I taught my students also got me a beautiful crystal vase. I thanked them and said that now I would have to buy some furniture. They laughed thinking that I was joking. Only I was not. In my apartment there is a mattress on the floor, a round table on a rusted leg in the kitchen and three chairs around it. Now I also have a crystal vase.

In this new land of mine there is no respect for anybody. In Greenwich Village you can purchase a roll of toilet paper with the faces of all American Presidents printed on it.

"Why don't stamps with Carter's portrait stick to the envelope? Because everybody spits on the wrong side." Well, how about fifteen years in Siberia for you and your whole family for telling such a joke? People in Russia have been shot for less. Here they tell such stories on radio and TV.

A joke. An old man on a plane is closely examining his neighbor, a young man in a weird hairdo. Both sides of a young man's head have been shaven leaving a strip of hair in the middle. The remaining hair smeared with jell is standing up and colored in many different colors. The young man becoming a little irritated at the extent that an old gentleman is visibly examining him asks him what is the problem. The old man says to him. "In my days I also did many crazy things. Once in California I even screwed a parrot. Who knows, maybe you're my son."

In Europe people try to look a little better than they actually are, and in America a little worse, and that a little bit makes a lot of a difference. There are quite a number of people in New York who've given up on being human. First they lost the last letter in the word "humane" and then the whole word went. This is not necessarily a New York phenomenon. I've seen such people in Europe too, but there they are aware that it is unnatural for a human being not to be human, and having ceased to belong to human species, they at least pretend that they still do belong. Not so in New York. Here all pretense has been dropped. As Pablo Neruda wrote 'I am tired of being a man;' the same way in this metropolis some are tired of being human. In the midst of crowds, excruciating noise, and filled with exhaust fumes in the air, among mice, rats, roaches, litter, empty soda cans, broken beer bottles and used condoms sprawled on the pavement, the desire has been born to become a part a different species, to crawl, growl, howl, bite and tear apart, grow fangs and tails and thus get licensed to eat, sleep, defecate, urinate and have sex right in the middle of the street in broad daylight, in view of everybody.

- How was your trip to New York?
- Fine, but there was one thing I didn't like.
- What was that?
- Roaches.
- Hum, roaches? In New York?
- Yes, even in the hotel.
- Have you complained?
- I sure did. I called the hotel manager and told him that there was a roach on my table.
- Well?
- He said he didn't believe me.
It's looking me in the eye. I said to him. He still wouldn't believe me. That's when the roach said to me, "Listen, pal, let me speak to this idiot."

Going down 23rd street I heard a mail carrier speaking on the intercom. "Mam, I can't make a delivery. There is a gentleman blocking the entrance." I turned my head. The mailman had a big box on wheels. Right in front of the entrance an unconscious young man was sprawled on the pavement in the pool of his own vomit. I am certain that no dog or cat would be allowed to lie there in such a condition.

As I was sitting in a little park near the 63rd Street "Y", I looked up. Framed in a brightly lit window of a health club under a neon sign a bald middle-aged man was lifting weights while frantically biking nowhere on a stationary bicycle.

In a tiny garden under the window a cute field mouse was busy running among the flowers. It looked so adorable within its element right in the midst of the monstrous pulsating Metropolis.

NEIGHBORS, FRIENDS, ENCOUNTERS AND EXPERIENCES

Living in New York you can learn a lot about how people from different cultures think and express themselves. I found that both Americans and Russians are equally competitive, yet will express their competitive side in a different way. Having learned about your accomplishment Americans will smile politely and say, "Oh, that's great." Russians, on the other hand, will make some remark to show that your accomplishment isn't really that great. Irish are very encouraging. Indians will praise you to the sky for any small accomplishment.

In Brooklyn our neighbors Avi and Shushana are a Jewish couple from Israel. They own a shop in Boro Park that sells everything from cups and plates to electrical appliances and are pretty successful. Tonight I come home beaming with pride. My first story has been published in the Café Solo magazine in California. As I come off the elevator I see Avi carrying a big basket filled with laundry.

- So what's new with you, Irina?
- Oh, I do have some great news, Avi. My story "Second Life" has been published in California.
- Hum, really? I didn't know that you also write.
- I do.
- What do you write, Irina?
- Short stories.
- Ahm, Shushana writes too, you know; she writes poems, beautiful poems. And our daughter Sandy also writes poems. It's a pity you can't read them; they are in Hebrew.
- Have they ever published anything?

- Oh, no, they don't bother with that stuff.

We share a cottage in Sag Harbor, Long Island with an Irish couple Mary and Peter. Mary is a petite shapely brunette. She is a teacher. Peter is in his late fifties, an engineer and an amazing athlete; he has been jogging all his life. As a matter of fact he jogs ten miles to work every morning. He also starts swimming early in the spring. I call him Mr. Superman.

Bruce and I are returning home from a bike ride. Peter is at the gate.

- Where have you two been today?

- South Hampton. (A town, which is located about ten miles away from Sag Harbor).

- Wow, I didn't know you bike so far. Good for you, guys.

I, of course, am full of myself.

Later in the week speaking to his wife Mary.

- You know, Mary, I hate biking down that road near the pond. The dogs bark so ferociously, I get scared.

- Oh, it's that road to which you turn at the gas station?

- Exactly.

- Yeah, Peter hates it too. He says that of all the roads he takes when he bikes here from Flushing this one is the worst. (Flushing is about seventy-five miles away from Sag Harbor.)

Sima and Boris are from Riga, Latvia. In Riga, before emigrating to US I gave Sima private English lessons. In spite of my futile attempts, the English language that she has learned is enough to be understood but will forever remain broken for it was born crippled. She comes up with the phrases like "I tell you true", which means, "I'll tell you the truth," "Do you know my double cousin?" which means, "Do you know my second cousin?" "He is a gay. She is inferior decorator," etc,... here in the States Sima and Boris who are about twenty years older than me have become my surrogate parents. Our friendship has been solidified by all the troubles that immigrants go through in a new country – loneliness, sense of isolation, lack of money etc, ... When Sima learned that a couple of my stories had been published in some magazines she insisted on reading them and I brought her the periodicals. She called me on the phone after reading them.

- How did you like my stories, Sima?

- One story I liked. One story I didn't understand. And one story was OK. So that's the way they have been published, with mistakes?

What mistakes?

- I thought I saw some as I was reading them.

Sima is looking at the photo of my house that we purchased in Long Island. It's a two-storied house with a big porch that includes fourteen windows.

- So that's your house?

- Yeah.

- What I don't like about this house is that there are so many windows.

- But that's how I like it, Sima.

- OK. (Giving up.)

In a yoga class at Shivananda Yoga Center in New York everybody has settled down on the floor for the final relaxation in Shiva Asana, "the corpse pose". Being near the window I watch a real corpse in a black plastic bag being carried by two men out of the building across the street.

I walk into a Russian Book store on Fifth Avenue, take a book off the shelf, open it and am immediately overwhelmed by nostalgia.

"Can I help you?" I hear the saleslady's voice behind my back.

"Thanks. I'm just looking."

"It is not allowed to read books in the store," she orders in a stern voice. This cures my nostalgia immediately, I put the book back on the shelf and I leave the store.

There is a sign on the car that reads, "Look no radio. Glove compartment is open. No nothing," another where the car window is broken says, "No radio. Get one."

On a car reads a bumper sticker, "Watch my ass not hers."

A part of the sidewalk has just been covered with a new coat of concrete. A set of empty garbage cans connected by a red ribbon has been set around it, so that nobody would trample on it. Yet there is already a set of footprints and even a signature. "Alex. Sept, 03."

Sitting on a bench on Sixth Avenue I watch a drug addict stop in the middle of the street and search for something in his big bottomless bag. While searching for it, he is falling asleep. He wakes up only to fall into the abyss of forgetting. Then he perks up, as if he were a mechanical toy that has just been re-wound, shakes his head, curses and marches briskly away.

The hardest part of getting out of New York is coming back.

Loneliness of an Immigrant

If the phone rings at midnight,
I don't pick it up,
For I know it is not for me.
There are only two of us in this world,
And you are in bed right beside me.

A young couple with a baby in a stroller is waiting for the light on the corner of Third Avenue and Forty-First Street. The parents are in their mid - twenties, tall, strong, lean and beautiful. The baby is adorable with a big head, on which thick black hair is standing up like fur. Isn't this wonderful I think with a tinge of jealousy to be so young, beautiful, in love and with such a cute baby. That's when the young father turns to his mate and says, "Carmen, do you know what day it is?"

A very heavy Russian woman in Brighton is making her rounds, breathing like a furnace. I wonder how she manages to breathe at all for the jogging suit she is wearing allows no room for expansion.

Homeless guys are expressing their defiance by crossing a busy Third Avenue against the light. They don't care about their own lives, or anyone else. They don't want their lives and can't give them away.

Bruce's co-worker Gennady went to his car early in the morning only to find that it had disappeared. After half an hour of a futile search, frustrated Gennady called the police who informed him that work was being done on the block right next to the place where he had parked his car the night before. They figured it had probably been moved by the construction company and told him that if he walks around the block, he might be able to find it. Gennady had spent half a day combing the neighborhood until he finally located it. His wife's bright scarf left on the back seat had alerted him. It was a rented car. After examining it he noticed that the left light was slightly damaged but then he remembered that it already had this damage when he got it from the rental company. Gennady decided to sue the builders anyway, "I'll sue them not for the damage to my car," he said angrily, "but for what they have done to my nervous system." "Tell Gennady to get a new nervous system," I suggested to Bruce.

On our trip to Philadelphia we stopped for lunch at a local diner in a small town. Black ladies and gentlemen came in from the church. The ladies were tall, beautiful, big sized, full-breasted women, dressed up like opera divas in bright elaborate dresses, wide brimmed hats and high-heeled shoes. The gentlemen wore suits, starched shirts and ties. One of the ladies looked particularly dramatic. In her big blue hat with feathers she was like some exotic creature from the rain forest. It seemed that at any moment she would rise above the table on which a plate with chicken bones was resting and start singing in a dark rich mahogany voice.

Oh, to find myself in Greenwich Village in New York on a summer day that isn't hot, but just right is like a blessing from heaven. From my bench I see a little farmer's market that has sprung up on the corner of a cobble stone street. Like a horn of plenty, the buckets on the tables are overflowing with green zucchini, yellow string beans, red tomatoes and purple eggplants. The sea of flowers, lilies, roses and marigolds covers another table. A lovely young woman in a long yellow silk skirt is choosing a bouquet of roses. A smiling young farmer is helping her, taking flowers out of the bucket, showing them to her, enjoying the beauty of a woman whose attention is engrossed by the flowers. Her lover, a young woman in jeans and a red T-shirt is watching the scene from afar resentfully and sullenly.

In Brighton Beach where there is a big senior citizen community, you can see some garishly made up old women, dressed in revealing bright outfits. Their half blind eyes are shaded by long artificial eyelashes. Their fingers crippled by arthritis resembling the stumps of an old tree, are crowned with long brightly painted nails. At dusk these creatures look more like young women playing the role of the elderly than old women pretending to be young chicks.

One of my students has introduced me to a friend of hers, a Russian cleaning lady. She was so beautiful, refined and well educated that if she came to clean my house, I would sit her down in a chair in the middle of the room and clean the whole house by myself.

My father sent me the picture of my mother, my sister Natasha and me. In the picture I am about thirteen, Natasha is about five. Our mother is wedged between us, her two daughters like a meteorite. Her small hostile eyes are set deep in her round face. There is no smile on her face, no attempt to present to the world her better side for there is no better side to her. My mother is one-dimensional. All there is, is right there before the viewer. "With the face like that she could single-handedly defeat Hitler," Bruce said examining the picture. "They only had to put up posters with this face in front of the German army and say, "This is what their women look like, now imagine the men," and the Germans would have decided to retreat and go and conquer some other place."

My mother had a morbid attachment to the memories of her hungry youth spent on the Black Sea. By the end of her life, enormously heavy, her body swollen with retained water, she liked to reminisce after a good dinner how during the WWII she subsisted almost entirely on lemons and sunflower seeds.

An overweight African American beggar in Brighton Beach is addressing every passing man and woman as "Mama, Papa." Nobody is paying him any attention. Upon hearing him an old man shuffling by comes up to the beggar and announces in a disgruntled tone, "I am not your father." "So man, you've got yourself a lottery ticket," the beggar responds calmly and continues chiming,"Mama, Papa."

On the billboard of a local college an invitation for the students to purchase tickets for Puccini Tosca in Metropolitan Opera reads the following, "Puccini's Tosca, one of the most popular operas, is a violent drama based on Victorien Sardou's hit play Tosca. The action of the play and the opera takes place in Rome between noon of June 17, 1800 and dawn of the following day, during which time all the major characters die violent deaths."

A movie ad at a local movie theater reads, "Get in, get out, get even."

Right after 9/11 occurred a Pakistani gas pump attendant seeing that Bruce has no American flag sticker on his car and who also has a swarthy complexion hands him a sticker with the following words, "Here, let me give you an American flag or like me you can be mistaken."

In the Soviet Union it was impossible to find anything in the store and everything had to be bought under the table.

The story goes about a customer who spends a day in pursuit of a zipper. All the stores he goes to are out of zippers. By the end of the day the tired man enters yet another store where he asks a salesman if they have a zipper and hears the familiar answer, "Sorry, no zippers." "Where is the nearest store, where I can find a zipper?" inquires the frustrated customer. "In Sweden," answers the phlegmatic salesman.

From the Soviet Union comes a generation of clothes addicts. My friend Sonya is this way. She is a tall woman with a lean body, always beautifully attired. Her heavy short-legged husband Pyotr, on the other hand, resents spending money on clothes, yet she always buys him the best clothes she can find. "Sonya, why are you buying Pyotr all this expensive stuff?" I ask her, "He doesn't appreciate the clothes you buy for him." "I know that but I have to appear with him before our friends and acquaintances, and therefore, he has to be dressed well."

A conversation with an elderly Russian neighbor.
- Hi, Sofi, how are you?
- Fine, fine, thank you.
- Fine, Sofi, that's in English. And how about in Russian?
- Azohen vei is in Russian.
- What's the matter, Sofi?
- It's age, my dear, that's the matter.

In Greenwich Village in the heat of the summer young women wearing light summer dresses with an open back and heavy black boots look like pale sprouts shooting out of heavy footwear. They make me think of cosmonauts walking on the moon. For some of these beautiful creatures their boots are the only thing that prevents their anorexic bodies from floating away into polluted gray city sky.

On our way to Long Island we pass a cemetery in Queens. I am surprised that from the car it looks like a gigantic hair brush with spokes made out of stone or sets of teeth that are badly in need of braces. There are no flowers. There is no space between the gravestones. It is dark and gray. In contrast a Latvian cemetery is a vast green space filled with trees, bushes, chirping birds and breathtakingly beautiful flowerbeds. In big cemeteries like the ones in Riga some graves are adorned with hauntingly graceful monuments. Amidst all this beauty the living and the dead meet one more time. It is the place, where the dead rest and the living contemplate.

Seeing my surprise my friend Uldis says," Yes, here cemeteries look quite different, the reason being that real estate in New York is so expensive that corpses have to be buried in an upright position." I swear that if it were not for the explosion of laughter from the back seat, I would have believed him.

Elena from Poland is a pedicurist and works in a saloon. She says that American ladies have two main topics of conversation: where to go for good food and how to lose weight. While working she has probably heard many other discussions but is unable to understand them for she knows very little English. When she doesn't understand what people are saying to her she responds with, "Isn't that wonderful!" The other day when one of Elena's clients told her that her husband had fallen off the ladder and broken his leg she responded in her familiar cheerful fashion, "Oh, isn't that's wonderful!"

This reminds me of my friend Boris who lives on the first floor of a big apartment building and is often visited by all kinds of solicitors. It's his first year in America and his English is so poor that more often than not he fails to understand what he is being offered. He has learned to answer to all the offers with "Thank you, I've already got one." The other day an exterminator knocked on his door asking him if there were any rats in his apartment. "Thank you, I've already got one," answered Boris politely.

A Russian friend of mine speaking to Bruce, on the phone,"It is nice to see your voice."

The following is announced with great pride. "My daughter is inferior decorator."

Or "We have just bought a condom in Riverside."

This is whispered, "He is a gay."

My student is raising his hand, he wants to know how the word "icy"is spelled. "Sure,"I say,"Come to the blackboard and I'll spell it for you."He comes to the blackboard and I spell the word,"AI,SI,YAI". He writes on the blackboard. "I see why."

In Brighton Russian babushkas who are sitting in their folding chairs near the entrances to their apartment houses are always debating the same question, "Was leaving their homeland and coming to America the right thing to do?" In the end they all agree with a sigh, "It's for the children."

In all the countries where I have traveled so far the three institutions that always look the same are schools, jails and hospitals.

Many Russian Jews are grasping the concept of kosher food. The other day I overheard a conversation between two Jews, one Russian, and another one American. The Russian Jew asked, "Ben, what would you eat if you lived in a place where there was no kosher food?" I couldn't make out the answer. Then I heard the Russian Jew ask, "And what if you lived in a place where there were only pigs, pigs, pigs?"

My friend's mother was very happy that her grandson was going to spend the summer in a religious camp in the Catskills. "There he will learn how to be a real Jew and eat kosher food," she kept saying while making cutlets for her beloved grandson. Yuri asked her if the meat she was making the cutlets from was kosher to which she replied that much to her regret she couldn't afford kosher meat but she always made sure the cutlets were packed in a bag that had a kosher stamp on it.

Andrei bought some canned meat at the supermarket, brought it home and ate it for lunch. When I came over to speak to his wife Anna, he was finishing his meal. All of a sudden he jumped up with a look of great concern on his face, ran to the garbage can and grabbed an empty can. "Ann, what have I just eaten?" he shouted, "it says "beef" here. This doesn't mean "svinina" (pork), does it?

One of my Moslem students described in class how murderers are punished in his country. A murderer is brought into a mosque where his crime is announced before the people and then he is beheaded. "I saw it myself," he said. "They took a sword and cut his head off. Here in America they put him in jail and within a year you see him back on the street. In my old country you know that he is not coming back. How is he gonna come back? Here is his head and here is body."

In Europe nudity is not exciting, unless it is activated i.e. it is there to seduce somebody. Not so in America. In the land of sexual revolution, nudity is a big issue. Once on my way home from a twenty-mile bike ride I was passing The Long Beach in Sag Harbor. The sun was low on the horizon and the blue waters of the bay looked very enticing. I was hot and longed to take a swim. There was one problem. It being after six o'clock, the only bathroom on the beach was closed and there was no place for me to change into my bathing suit. The beach being absolutely flat there was no place to hide either, so I walked to a secluded area where I was completely alone and started changing, hoping that my over sized T-shirt was long enough to cover me. As I was pulling on my bathing suit I heard a voice coming from a passing truck, "Nice ass, lady."

LIFE IN THE BIG APPLE

Morning on the Subway

The sight of very young children on a morning subway train in New York makes me sad. They are torn out of sleep like pages out of a book. Full of dreams they are standing with their eyes closed in the middle of the train holding to a pole, protected from a three hundred legged herd by their parent or hanging listlessly on his shoulder. I imagine being a four or five year old, waking up to the sea of Monday morning faces on a subway train. Oh, the horror of it.

It's eight o'clock on a soggy October morning. I am on the B train going to Manhattan on my way to work. There is a woman with a child sitting on a bench. Her child is in a stroller by her side. It's not the first time I have seen them. Since they always have a seat, I figure they must be getting on the train at the end of the line. The morning crowds of New Yorkers are not generous about giving their seats to mothers with young children or the elderly. The woman is reading a book. Her daughter is a cute four-year old girl whose thick dark hair is gathered in a short ponytail on the top of her head making her look like a little pumpkin. She has beautiful dark eyes framed in thick eyelashes and a peachy complexion that a drop of Spanish blood has brought to her face. The girl is cranky from being up and out of the house at such an early hour. For them to be on the train at eight o'clock in the morning she must have been out of bed at seven. The mother is in her mid thirties, well built, in jeans and a jacket, her hair rolled up in a bun. She has well balanced features and would be considered good-looking if she were alive. However, she is dead tired. Her resentful eyes are framed in deep brown circles; her complexion is yellowish from fatigue. "Mommy, I want my book," the girl starts whining, "mommy, my book." Lost in her thoughts, the woman does not hear her. Her thoughts are about her man, the child's father. Her hostile glance traces the man's features on the little pumpkin face, his determined chin, his turned up nose. There's no peace when he is around and when he is away, his child takes over. Eventually he too will leave like all the others before him. They all do. They come, do their thing and then go leaving their children behind. Her oldest is sixteen. Her welfare benefits are running out in six months. She doesn't know how it all started or how to end it. All she knows is that now she's got to go out and provide for their children. Men come and go and all that's left is this tremendous resentment and tiredness. All she wants is sleep, sleep, sleep. Her puffed eyelids start coming down on her watery reddish eyes. "Mommy, give me my book," the girl is asking, "my book, mommy, my book!!" The child's screams penetrate her mother's stupor. Like a sleepwalker she reaches into her bag and hands her daughter a book. The child opens it and immediately throws it on the floor. The mother bends down, picks the book up and puts it back in her bag. "Mommy, give me my doll," the child is pleading, "Mommy, my doll." The woman is looking at her with a far away look. She is thousands of miles away. Suddenly her face softens, she picks her daughter up from the stroller with the part of her that is still alive and sits her in her lap. Her dead part is watching. I picture the woman's apartment with a window facing a wall, cockroaches in the kitchen sink, and dusty faded plastic roses in a glass vase. Maybe she can still be resurrected. If only there was a room with a bed and clean sheets where she could stretch out her tired body and get some sleep, for she needs her sleep the way a thirsty plant needs water, but this is one thing she is not going to get.

THE SUBWAY

Somebody has posted yellow strips of paper with "Jesus help me" written on them all over the subway stops in downtown Brooklyn. The strips which were left loose at one end are brought to life by the breath of in-coming trains. They tremble in the wind, flutter and rustle. Seconds later a dragon of a train rolls out of the dark tunnel breathing sparks, sounding like a monstrous empty can. "Jesus help me," so many of them. Wherever I go, the strips are there. Seeing them, defenseless and alive in the wind brings sadness to my soul and I say a prayer for the hand that has written them, say it without words, just with my overflowing sadness.

The heavy stale air of the subway smells of human waste. Two men leaning over the edge of the platform are watching mice running across the tracks. One of them says, "Shi-i-it, look how they run," and they both laugh.

THE TRAIN

The New York subways make me think of a mortally wounded beast that stubbornly refuses to drop dead. The beast does so defying every law of nature, and its moving ahead is a pure act of will. At times it runs in delirious agony for a couple of minutes but quickly gets out of breath, exhausted by such thoughtless expenditure of energy, slows down and hardly moves for the next half hour. Then a shudder runs through its entire body and with a deep sigh of resignation, as if its every bone was in excruciating pain, it stops for five to ten minutes. This may lead you to believe that it has finally dropped dead between the stops. Even though you are hopelessly late, the silence brings you relief – for it means that at least its suffering, if not yours, has come to an end. But lo and behold, the beast picks itself up once again with a low mournful sigh of an old arthritic man getting out of a deep armchair, only to collapse seconds later.

This agony of the New York subways reminds me of that famous scene in Hamlet, when Hamlet has already been wounded by a poisoned weapon. He is still moving, but is no longer alive, and he and the spectator know it.

Today is one of those mornings when a forty-five minute subway ride is threatening to stretch into an hour and a half of torture. This man gets on the train a stop after me. He is agitated and upset. He runs up and down the aisle, cursing and talking to himself. As the train fills up more and more at each stop, he has less and less space to move in and his agitation increases accordingly. He mumbles, "What a weekend! Oh, what a weekend!" He waves his hands helplessly like a broken bird. His lower lip hangs down like an open flap of a purse, revealing a row of big yellow canine teeth. His face wears the sign of insanity. He is late and the train refuses to move. The man is trying to talk it into closing its doors. He threatens it, he pleads with it, moans and curses, but to no avail. The train just won't move.

On Ocean Parkway a man with Down Syndrome enters the car. After a few minutes of watching the disturbed man's agitation he says loudly and firmly, " Mike, calm down! Calm down, Mike! The N train is just two stops away. You can change for the N train on 36th Street if you want to." It works. Mike turns to him and a faint shadow of recognition passes his face. "It's okay," he says. "Don't worry. I'll calm down. It's okay. I don't want to change. I'll stay on this train. It's o'kay. I'll relax." For a while he manages to calm down. But it doesn't last long, for as soon as the man with Down Syndrome gets off the train, and Mike gets squeezed into a small space near a pole by three women, his agitation erupts. He reaches for his private parts and starts shaking. However, his body, just like that of the train, is lacking in energy and he gets distracted.

I turn my eyes to an ad above the window. The ad is in Spanish. It depicts scattered Coca Cola cans and paper cups with rats drinking out of them. You see their heavy behinds, long tails and thin legs. It must be something about littering. Now Mike's face is lightly touching the long hair of a young woman who is standing with her back to him. His hand is on his private parts. He is shaking, his eyes half closed and his mouth wide open. There is an expression of longing and pain on Mike's face. This is perhaps the closest he has ever been to a woman. The young lady tries to see who is behind her. She turns her head slightly from side to side like a frightened animal, gets a glimpse of Mike and turns her face away. Her thick luxurious hair runs loose on her shoulders, a cheap emerald earring sparkles in her pink ear. She is fragile and vulnerable. Everybody is observing the scene, some with disgust, others with surprise, but for most passengers it's just a distraction from the subway situation, which is getting worse with every stop.

The train puffs, moans and sighs, apologizes for inconvenience and thanks passengers for their cooperation. In short, all the signs that generally precede its death-resurrection scene are present. Some passengers get off at the next station, and the woman with the sparkling emerald earrings gets a seat. Of the two women sharing the pole with Mike now, one is an ice-cold Caucasian executive type, the other is an Asian whose firmly closed eyelids make her face look like a death mask. I turn my eyes back to the rat ad and plead for my stop to come, for all of a sudden I feel as if I were in deep water and my lungs are going to collapse from lack of air. Soon, very soon, I am saying to myself, I'll get off at the bus terminal, run along the endless corridor, past a classical record shop, where, opposite from the sounds of noble symphonies, people covered with rags will be sleeping on the floor or begging for money.

Then I'll go up the escalator onto the main street and pass the soup kitchen where a policeman will be directing a long line of people waiting for their morning meal, then onto the crossroad where squeegees wash the windows of the cars that stop for the red light. Some drivers will open the window and give a squeegee a dollar, others will take off as soon as the light changes followed by the loud and angry "Fuck you!" Sometimes I see a squeegee urinate into a container and then wash the car windows with his own urine.

I'll cross the wide Third Avenue and will be greeted at the door by our Rumanian doorman. It's his sixth month in America. He doesn't know much English and he's homesick and sad. "How is the weather today?" He asks slowly and with difficulty; every word is such a heavy and awkward commodity for him. We have a joke between us that he is in charge of the weather as well as security. "Fine, the weather is fine," I'll answer with a smile and take the elevator to the sixth floor. When the elevator door opens, the clock on the wall will say ten to nine. The poster under the clock will read. "It's Monday morning and let the stress begin."

A NEW SPECIES HAS BEEN BORN

The thing about New York is that there are too many people who totally gave up on being human.

I am not saying that it is necessarily a NY phenomenon. I've seen people like these not in such numbers in Europe, however, they have the desire, the energy at least to pretend that they belong to the human species.

Not so in NY. Here all pretense has been dropped. As Pablo Nerudo wrote: "I am tired of being a man." We become tired of being human. The destruction of the family and lack of social interaction contributed to this phenomenon.

So in the midst of crowds, excruciating noise, packed tight trains, and purple from exhaust and polluted city air, amidst mice, rats, cockroaches, and used condoms lying on the pavement with litter, empty cans of soda, broken bottles, a new species has been born called New Yorkers.

A POOL OF MILK

There is a pool of milk on a seat on the 'A' train. An old lady sits down in the next seat and puts her shopping bag down right in it. "Shall I tell her?" Bruce asks me. I notice her faded gray coat and the look of irritation and resentment that so many New Yorkers wear upon entering the subway and one day just forget to take off. I imagine that if he calls her attention to it she would pretend not to hear him: then, being unable to ignore him any longer, she would turn her head and her fear would prevent her from understanding him. She may well be deaf too, so he'll have to shout, which would attract everybody's attention. The moment of fear she'll have to endure is not worth saving her sloppy shopping bag, which is already wet anyway.

So I tell him: "Don't."

"Why not?" Bruce is surprised. I provide him with my logic, which is if somebody spills milk on the seat then it's somebody else's lot to wipe it up.

With that in mind we watch the Pool slowly disappear, getting slowly absorbed by the green shopping bag. When the old lady finally gets up and slowly walks to the door, she leaves drops of milk all over the aisle. One of the drops settles on the sneakers of a young lady in jeans and windbreaker. The girl reminds me of a frostbitten fruit. She is in her mid-twenties with a face that is already marked by bitterness. I watch the peculiar absent look in her eyes, whose lids are bluish and heavy with fatigue. She is munching on a rice cake. As she chews, her jaws move rhythmically. It seems that she is not eating, just putting some fuel in her tired mechanism. The rice cake she bites into is making dry scratchy foodless sounds. The remaining milk is now absorbed by a young man's coat. Clearly he sat on it while my interest was elsewhere. Bruce following my previous instructions, watches the scene in silence. The man and his wife who has warm eyes and a golden ring with a pearl on her finger take turns peeking inside a paper bag. They just made a good buy at Delancey Street. They look Russian to me... and they sound it too. My own people soaking in a pool of milk! But is too late. The young wife will have to wash the milk stain off tonight.

The train is pulling into 23rd Street. We are getting off. Bye.

DINNER WITH OLENKA

Last Friday Olenka and I went to The Golden Dragon on Nostrand Avenue. We had Buddha's Delight, Shrimp, rice and laughs, good laughs. I told her my analyst said I had a neurosis. "You, a neurosis?" she said. "What kind of neurosis?" "I believe there are no men left, and Dr. Greenberg says it's my neurosis." We started giggling, a low dignified giggle, which grew to hysterics. "It almost seems," she said gasping for air, that to think otherwise would be a neurosis." "Where did Shirley MacLaine go to see those spaceships? To Peru? That's where I have to go. If I can't get myself a man, maybe I can get a Martian."

A tall lean couple in their late thirties sat down at the next table. A waiter brought them a huge mountain of white rice. I wondered what dish that was.

- "What have you been doing with yourself lately?" I heard the tall red head say.

- "Keeping pretty much to myself." Her balding companion responded.

-"Me too. That's what everyone seems to be doing these days."

The red head stared at the passers-by through the window. A light rain started and many colorful umbrellas bloomed on the street. Who were these people, neither friends nor lovers with a mountain of rice floating, like a gigantic iceberg in the ocean of emptiness between them? With her beetle neck, which accentuated her flat chest and her red hair brushed back, she looked sexless. Whose fault was it? The man's sitting across the table, life's, or her own?

- "I've been married to Richard for fourteen years," sighed Olenka. "This tall guy in my class asked me out for a drink."

- "Well?"
- "I didn't go."
- "Why not?"
- "I'm not looking for trouble."

We paid the bill and left. It was getting dark. I headed for the subway, the M line.

"Hi," I heard a deep velvet voice roll deeply over my shoulder. I looked back. It was a burly black fellow with a shiny bald head.

- "Peace," he said quickly, "peace. People are scared nowadays, you know."
- "I know."
- "My name's Andrew."
- "Hi, Andrew."
- "Look, here's my license. You see, it says, "Good until 2008. I'm a cab driver. I just had it renewed. Now you know that I'm qualified to talk with you. I have a license. I like to talk sometimes."
- "Andrew," I said. "I'm married with three kids."
- "That's all right," he said. "I'm married myself... Have been for the last twenty years. No harm in talking. I often walk here by myself in the evening. No people. Nobody's bothering me. What's your name?
- "Tatyana."
- "Pleased to meet you, Tatyana."
- "Likewise."
- "Thanks for talking with me."
- "All right."
- "Do you live here?"
- "Nope."
- "Then you must work here."
- "Uh-huh."
- "Will I see you some day?"
- "Maybe."
- "Where are you headed now, dear? Home?"
- "Yes."
- "To the subway?"
- "Uh-huh."

I started down the steps.

- "Bye, Andrew."

- "Bye, Tatyana. Thank you."
- "My pleasure."
He leaned over the banister and waved. I waved back.

The M train came. Halfway home the train broke down. We got out and had to wait for the next one for twenty minutes. Standing there on the outside platform, I savored the taste of laughter on my lips. It was dark. Rain had finally washed the city's September air clean, so clean. In the distance the lights were pulsating, full, alive and breathing. I looked at my watch. It was 8:30 PM.

A MAD MAN

On a partition between the tracks
a dark coat is lying
like a shriveled human form.

A mad man is pacing back and forth
examining his sweater
and talking to himself incessantly.
His words keep seeping through my ears
like water through a broken bucket.
He's talking to himself in such a calm and gentle fashion,
as if he were in his kitchen
shuffling between a table and a sink
preparing his dinner.
Yet, I can't make out what he is saying.

A Peruvian band of three boys
with faces from a far away land
is playing a warm and tender song
which rises
above the stench, the vomit and the noise
of the city subway.
It wakes such sadness and longing in my heart
for the colors, shapes and smells
of the land that it has come from.
"How did it get here?" I ponder.
Like a bright bird that flew into a flat
through a narrow space
between a curtain and a window pane,

it knows it cannot stay here.
How will it get back?
Or will it grow crazy with desperation,
assume a human form that'll start examining its sweater
while talking to itself
until the monstrous subway
sucks out its trembling flesh
and drops its empty peel
on a partition
between the tracks?

The sadness in my heart keeps growing,
fills up my lungs
and gets stuck in my throat.
It's difficult to breathe.

SHOPPING AT BRIGHTON WITH RAYA

Raya, a scrawny little woman looks like a teenage boy rather than a forty-four year old wife and a mother of two grown kids. Skinny, with bushy reddish hair, she is quick in both her speech and her actions. Opposites do attract, so we've become good friends. I am a tall, slow and a deliberate no-nonsense woman, one of those whom guys standing on the corner call "Big mama" with respect and admiration.

Now that Raya and her family has moved to Staten Island and we've got separated by a bridge and a toll, we do not get to see each other too often but before this unfortunate event took place we used to spend much time together and among other things we would shop at Brighton once or twice a week.

Brighton Beach Avenue lies near the ocean and has an endless row of Korean markets that exhibit all shapes and colors of voluptuous fruit, berries and vegetables. It took me some time to learn their names, for having come out the Soviet Latvia, I knew little more than the sight and taste of oranges, lemons, tangerines and an occasional grapefruit.

I am amused by the small, round, firm and furry kiwi, the clumsy enormity of a succulent ugly fruit, the rough brownness of a Chinese pear, the heavenly taste of violet figs and the all pervading sweet smell of a honey dew, not to mention a delicate coral persimmon, a strange yellow fruit called Star that looks like a plastic toy and a nutty butterish avocado shaped like a dark green grenade. The only remaining mystery is the seemingly inedible roots of enormous size and strength displayed in Haitian markets. About twice a week we would get drunk on all these shapes, smells and colors and bring home bags of vegetables and fruits.

It would usually work in the following way. I would meet Raya at Brighton and we would go shopping. After the shopping was done, she would leave me near a stall surrounded by numerous bags, and run to fetch her car parked somewhere around the corner. Let me tell you, that woman did not know how to walk. All she could do was run or fly. I would be standing there like a devoted dog wagging its tail at every approaching car, for there were three beat-up cars in her family and I never knew which one she chose to drive on any particular day. The moment she would appear and honk her horn impatiently, I would grab two or three of the largest bags and quickly make my way to the car. The reason for such haste was in Raya's bad back that she had developed from working as a nurse in the home for the elderly. That's why I would always try to save the heaviest bags for myself. On the other hand, Raya would insist on carrying the biggest bags for she was the one with a big family which consisted of a husband and two children and as a rule the biggest bags belonged to her. Thus, there was always a silent struggle for the heaviest bags going on between us.

So it was this time, when I heard Raya's neurotic horn I instantly grabbed the two biggest bags and ran to the car. On that particular day I considered my efficiency to be of crucial importance for I had noticed the grimace that Raya wore when her back was acting up. I saw my task as not only putting the heaviest bags into the trunk, but also saving the two remaining bags with a watermelon and potatoes for myself. She could have the rest. This was not an easy task though for as I had told you before, I am a big and slow woman and the bags were rather heavy and bulky. As I was throwing the first two bags into the trunk of the car, I saw Raya's foot emerge from the car.

I turned around and assessed the situation. Between me and the remaining bags there was a bus shelter in which I noticed a missing panel of glass. If I squeezed myself through this narrow opening I would save time and get to the bags first. Quickly I ran to the bus stop shelter and squeezed myself through the narrow space of the missing glass. Half of me was already outside when my foot got caught on the rail that was holding the panels together and my entire six foot frame went down with a thump.

I swear I had never even brushed against the old guy who was carefully shuffling on his way along the sidewalk between the bus shelter and the bags, but as if thrown by an explosion at the sight of me falling down, he backed up and landed on a sack of tomatoes belonging to a street vendor.

When I got back on my feet I saw Raya already at his side. Of course she got there first and was now displaying every sign of professional attention. She was checking his pulse, patting his arm and asking him if he had been hurt in any way.

To my surprise the old man was exhibiting no sign of discomfort. Lying on his back on the sack of tomatoes he was saying something in Italian and slowly turning his head from side to side. I followed his glance. On his right there were voluptuous juicy peaches and yellow pears with a delicate blush. On his left there were tropical flowers of every shade and shape. Right above him there was this enormous blue sky with a lonely bird circling in it. "He must think he is in heaven," I whispered in Raya's ear. The old man looked like he was trying to comprehend the strange sequence of events that had landed him on the sack of tomatoes. He had lived a long life in the course of which he had witnessed many strange events. Things had fallen on him from behind, from in front of him, from above, but nobody had ever fallen on him from out of a bus stop shelter. It must have been through divine intervention that he got catapulted right into the Garden of Eden.

In the meantime, the tiny Korean grocer and his assistant were running around conversing excitedly in the strange sounds of Korean language, obviously concerned about their produce. They were like two desperate birds whose nest was being invaded. Finally, they carefully raised the old man and gently put him back on his feet. He looked around in surprise and calmly shuffled on his way paying no attention to my frantic apologies.

While I stood there numb in the middle of the street watching him walk away, Raya darted to the remaining bags, grabbed the two biggest ones and ran straight to the car. To tell you the truth, at that moment I was so shook up I didn't even care.

A TRIP TO MANHATTAN

On a hot hazy summer afternoon we left the Indian museum and went to the walkway along the Hudson River that leads right into the World Trade Center. There were twelve of us – two teachers, Natalie and me, our tutor Connie, and nine students from Kingsboro College. It was a relief to be near the water after such a scorching day. The wide walkway allowed a lot of human traffic. Joggers ran past us, young fathers paraded their babies in strollers, well dressed women walked their well-groomed dogs, among which there were many funny looking poodles whose fur was cut as if they were some exotic bushes. Most of the people were from Wall Street and everything about them from the tip of their foreign made shoes to fashionable haircuts spoke of money and power. They seemed to be immune to hot weather and didn't look at all uncomfortable in their suits, starched shirts and ties on such a hot stifling afternoon. I, on the other hand, longed to jump right into the river, no matter how dirty it looked, with empty cigarette boxes and soda cans floating in its dark polluted waters. Along the concourse in open restaurants under colorful umbrellas customers were having dinner and sipping iced tea from tall glasses. It all was very different from what our students were used to in their Brooklyn neighborhoods and they observed the rich Manhattan scene with interest.

Natalie was walking a little ahead of everybody. Usually so talkative, today she appeared to be lost in thoughts, her head lowered, looking at the ground. All of a sudden I saw her almost collide with a tall slim man in sneaks and a jogging outfit who was jogging along the concourse with his female companion. Natalie stopped and apologized. The gentleman flashed his golden - rimmed glasses at her and said that he too was sorry, after which they butted against each other and neither one would give way. "Aren't you going to let me pass?" asked Natalie. "You, women, are the ones who want equality in everything," said the annoyed gentleman, "so why should I be the one to let you pass?

You'll have to step aside and walk around me" "C'mon, I am too old for this crap," responded Natalie, a short, stocky, balding Jewish woman in her mid fifties. The man shrugged his shoulders, took The New York Times out of his pocket, unfolded it and started reading it. In response, Natalie took a thick book out of her black leather pocketbook and also started reading it. If anything, Natalie was bound to win because she was reading a thick book and all the man had to occupy himself with was The New York Times, the weekday edition, you know, which could be finished in an hour. The rest of us stood there silently watching the whole scene and then with a long sigh settled down on the nearby bench. We were hot, tired and wanted to go home. His woman companion, a pale blond woman of about forty sat down on the bench too. "Sam," she said to the man, "you are an idiot." "You see," Natalie said pointing at her and looking at the man through her ultra-fashionable gold rimmed glasses, "even she knows that." The man exhibited no reaction whatsoever and continued reading the newspaper. After about fifteen, twenty minutes some of us were beginning to feel quite anxious. Connie asked one of the students, Jimmy Karpov for a cigarette. I had never seen her smoke before, but there she was puffing away like a real pro. Another ten minutes passed and I saw the jogger and Natalie exchange a couple of words after which the man smiled at her politely, and stepped aside letting her pass. "What has happened?" I asked her as she was triumphantly trotting towards us. "Well, he asked me where I was working and I said at the college. Then he asked me if I was a teacher and I said, yes I was. As a matter of fact I was teaching right now, I said pointing at you guys sitting on the bench." "Oh," he said, "I'll give way to Academia," and he let me pass." As we were getting off the walkway we saw the couple jogging past us again. The man smiled at Natalie flashing at her his golden-rimmed glasses.

ONE MAN BAND

Every morning, this black guy sits in a long subway corridor under 42nd Street, and sings into a microphone. When he presses his foot down, he sets cymbals in motion, and a simple mechanism brings them together. When he's not singing he's playing a harmonica which is attached to the microphone while his hands keep busy while strumming the guitar.

The man releases so many sounds into the air, which smells of chlorine and human waste, that at first you might think there's a small band playing, until, of course, you round the corner and come into full view of him and his many instruments.

His face is always shadowed by a big felt hat, and, whatever little of it remains exposed to the observer, has an impersonal, impenetrable look. That's the way he wants to appear-as part of a musical machine.

In front of him sits an open guitar case. People rushing to the trains throw loose change into it. Silver coins and copper pennies glimmer on its dark purple velvet. If you pass him early in the morning, when he's a little stiff after a night's sleep, you can tell that it is not always easy for him to coordinate his movements. I judge how late I am for work by how smoothly he is playing. Today, for example, the train got stuck in the tunnel, and I could tell it was getting late for he was warmed up, the country song was flowing effortlessly, without any pauses.

As I approach him, I see that he has a spectator. It is a middle-aged black lady, poorly yet neatly clad, with her hair pleated in two curved-up pigtails. She is slim, and in her dark coat, she appeared younger than her years. She is standing there, watching and listening, transfixed like a spellbound five-year old. Observing his every move, she reminds me of a cat glued to the glass aquarium.

The musician apparently not used to having such a devoted audience, is amused by her presence. All he sees from under his large hat is a pair of heavy, dark brown shoes weighing down her thin legs. He tilts his head a little to get a glimpse of his fan. Realizing her fascination, his face lost its impenetrable cool, and he flashes a most bashful childish smile. But she either doesn't notice, or cannot respond, and simply continues standing there immersed in the happening.

Pushing through the turnstile, I realize I am late again. The gate clock reads 9:15.

THANK GOD IT IS FRIDAY

I doze off on a Brooklyn train. I must have slept for a while, for when I open my eyes we are already approaching Delancey Street. Right across from me there is a fine specimen of black manhood with proudly chiseled features. The man is in his mid twenties, dressed in jeans and a leather jacket with a bright red woolen scarf wrapped around his neck.

The young man's body is slightly tilted forward as if forever frozen in a fight or flight response. He is taking stock of his surroundings, for he knows the world as a dangerous place where one must take no chances and be ready for anything at any time. All of a sudden his face assumes a surprised expression, which quickly changes into a hostile one. I follow his glance.

The recipient is a plump Hasidic boy of about fifteen, dressed in black. His huge hat oddly perched on his yarmulke looks like a crow that is ready to take off at any moment. Under the hat is a face, framed in payees whose pale cheeks with a delicate blush make me think of cream, rising dough and blooming cherry trees. His eyes are shortsighted blue pools of innocence under his awkward, heavily framed glasses.

The black man seems to be wondering how such a phenomenon is allowed to exist and dares to share his space. He examines the young man closely. At the same time the Hasid, who is totally unaware of such close interest in his persona, is also curiously examining his fellow passengers through his awkward heavy glasses. In doing so, he turns his head to the left, clumsily stumbles into the black man's hostile glance and freezes in it for a moment as if hypnotized. Then he dismisses it and slips back into his knowledge of a world as a safe and amicable

SATURDAY NIGHT AT A BAGEL SHOP

There are many coffee shops in the Village. Now some of them are going out of business but the place where we with Bruce like to meet which is located near the corner of the Avenue of Americas has survived so far. Here you can always count on a simple dish like three bean salad or a cup of green pea soup and apple pie. It's a clean place where you can sip dark hot coffee out of a paper cup and watch people go by. No one rushes you.

Today we with Bruce are meeting here after work. I get there at a quarter to six and pay for a cup of tea and a bagel. All tables by the window being taken I settle down at the back of the store. It's five to six. Slowly snow starts falling. From the back of the store and framed by the window lights, the sight of the snow and the people rushing by holding on to their colorfully wrapped gift boxes, looks like a scene on a Christmas card. When Bruce walks through the door, his shoulders and beret covered with snow make him look both taller and bulkier than he actually is. He waves to me, goes to the counter and brings to the table a tray with a bagel and a steaming cup of coffee. Having brushed off the melting snow, he takes his jacket off, sits down and hungrily sinks his teeth into the toasted poppy bagel with tuna salad.

That's when right behind me I hear a loud voice and turn around. The voice belongs to a wiry guy in jeans and a black leather jacket leaning over the counter. "I've just lost seventy-five cents in your phone and I want my money back," he says," Somebody here must accept responsibility." The workers behind the counter shrug their shoulders. The phone is on the other side of the store and as far as they are concerned it might as well be on the other side of the galaxy. The man turns up a volume, "I am not leaving until I get my money back, understand? Last week I lost a quarter and walked away. This time it's seventy-five cents and I'm not walking away with nothing."

After the initial surprise the customers lose their interest in the dispute. A young mother with a child moves the stroller out of the way so that it wouldn't get overturned if a fight breaks out and then resumes her conversation with a short plump girl in a blue felt hat and glasses. A heavy-set man at the third table from the window is lazily sipping his coffee and leafing through the Sunday times magazine. A withering blond in front of us begins to repair her make-up. The guy in the leather jacket looks around as if calling for witnesses to his injustice and is hurt by such lack of attention. "Give me my money back or I"ll trash this place!" he shouts and starts banging his fist on the counter.

The young mother straightens her hat and places her hand on the stroller prepared to flee at any moment. The hefty man folds his magazine and positions his body so that he can view the scene in comfort. The girl in a blue felt hat puts the mirror back into her bag and re-establishes glasses on her formidable nose. The countermen consult with each other; then with the piercing scream,"You want the police?" one of them jumps at the guy and tries to push him away from the counter. But the young man is much stronger than his sparse body suggests and he puts on a struggle in which a milk container, packages of straws, napkins and paper cups are knocked over. The milk spills out on the floor forming a big white puddle; red and blue straws scatter around it. Another short burly worker hurries from behind the counter to help in the fight, while a young boy in a white jacket and apron all smeared with tomato sauce runs out of the kitchen to the phones to call the police.

At the same time, a middle aged woman in a tightly fitting dress and false eyelashes, glides past the running worker into the store. She looks at the struggling trio, smiles coquettishly at the man behind the counter who politely if somewhat tensely returns her smile and orders two toasted bagels with cream cheese to go. Customers continue to trickle in with take out orders. Another worker hurries out of the kitchen to help at the take out counter. All this is happening to the accompaniment of the grunts, thuds and heavy breathing of the fighters on the floor. For a time they managed to keep the man pinned down, when all of a sudden he emits a blood thirsty scream and the fighting breaks out again. More cups and napkins fly up in the air. Chairs are overturned. Silverware is clanging. One of the workers pounces on him and starts strangling him.

The young mother jumps onto her feet and maneuvers her stroller out of the coffee shop, others follow her in quick step. Everybody manages to get past the fighters unscathed and now people are congregating near the entrance looking anxiously for the police car to come by. A siren is heard. No luck. It's only an ambulance.

All of a sudden, the hefty man spots a cop driving down the street. The car stops for a red light. He runs towards it waving his magazine as a flag at the cop. The cop gets out of the police car and they both hurry towards the coffee shop. The cop is a middle aged man with a little paunch and a gun on his belt. The hefty man is puffing behind him, briefing him on the situation. The cop enters the store. The hefty man stays outside. Breathing heavily he pulls out his handkerchief and wipes his face.

At the sight of the cop running in, the crowds that mill through the streets of the Greenwich Village on a warm Saturday night in search of things to do, follow him into the coffee shop. Seeing that no blood has been spilled and the fighters have picked themselves up from the floor and are straightening their clothes, they are disappointed. A drag queen with died copper hair gathered in a ponytail swings his hips provocatively and jingles an enormous golden earring as he walks off saying in a low husky provocative voice, "Oh, let's get out of here before we all get hu-u-urt." The others follow. So do we.

Forty minutes later, we pass the place again. Customers are sitting at the dimly lit tables sipping their coffee. "How much did you pay for your bagel and coffee?" I ask Bruce. "Three bucks." he says. "Well, you've got your money's worth," I say as we walked into the subway.

SATURDAY NIGHT AT A NIGHT CLUB

We arrived at the nightclub an hour and a half before the performance. A pretty, full-lipped, high heeled hostess led us to our table. We found ourselves in a hall decorated by two fake palm trees, one of which spread its huge cardboard branches right over our heads. Two or three couples were cautiously testing the waters of the dance floor, conscious of many eyes resting on them. Most of the men wore suits. As for the women, some were dressed as if they had just stepped out of the office. Their pants and somber uninspiring blouses were a testimony to their disinterest in their attire. Then there were those who were wearing open glittering dresses, expensive jewelry and high-heeled shoes.

Efficient waiters in green shirts darted from one end of the enormous hall to the other, like a swift fish in a moonlit pond. One of them surfaced by our side and we ordered a fancy pizza and couscous. When the order arrived, the pizza was too dry and spicy and the couscous, watery and bland. On top of the couscous unidentified veggies rested limply in a heap.

It was ten o'clock. The place was quickly filling up with people. The violet rivulets of cigarette smoke were beginning to tickle my nostrils. Amplified by two enormous speakers on both sides of the stage, the music assumed a palpable quality. It was angrily throwing itself against the walls and hot sweaty bodies were trying to escape this confinement. A white couple stepped out onto the dance floor. They tried moving to calypso music but just couldn't. The harder they tried, the more they failed. They covered their embarrassment with animated conversation. At times, they'd stop dancing as if overcome by some compelling topic. Stubbornly they refused to sit down even though their awkward bodies would not move to calypso music. I observed that

173

while other dancers' movements were horizontal and originated in midsection, theirs stiffly coursed up and down, affecting only their upper bodies. The girl was helplessly swaying her long skinny arms and her partner's jerky movements were painful to watch.

At a long table where a birthday party was being celebrated, a handsome Cuban man of about twenty-two sat facing me. His eyes reflected the silent suffering of a caged animal. I could see that the music was getting to him, too. Some of the women with high-pitched voices managed to sustain a semblance of a conversation. Not me. When the time came to announce my departure to the ladies' room, I had to scribble it on a napkin.

More and more people were arriving. The small white tables were lost in the hall, tiny boats bobbing among the vast sea of human bodies. It bothered me that my elbow often invaded the territory of the total stranger on my left who came in about forty minutes after us, sat down in silence and ordered a veal cutlet, well done. It obviously was no better than our couscous, for he left half of his meager portion on his plate.

In the meantime, a birthday cake arrived at the birthday table. In the semi-darkness of the hall, the two sparklers stuck in it, shone brightly. No matter how skillfully the waiter tried to maneuver the erupting cake, there not being an inch free from human flesh, its cold piercing sparkles were landing on ladies' naked shoulders and gentlemen's starched shirts. Finally, to everybody's relief, the cake was placed in the middle of the table, a birthday song was sung and a man with a camera took a few snapshots.

At half past eleven I noticed some movement on the stage. The musicians were coming on. They were West Indians. Some of them wore their hair braided and tied into something resembling a kitchen mop. I was hoping for some relief when they started playing, but it didn't happen. To my ear their music sounded pretty much like the one that had come out of merciless speakers. The crowd was of a different opinion. People sprang onto their feet and began swaying rhythmically to the music. As soon as everybody got up, it became obvious that the place was dangerously overcrowded.

Meantime, a short white girl in a cute yellow hat climbed on the stage. She was followed by a young Spanish man. As she turned around, she revealed enormous breasts scantily covered by a short sleeveless pink top.

She wore no bra. First, she swayed her breasts to the music. Then she, the Spanish guy and the singer started dancing together. She was rubbing her voluptuous bosom against the singer's back while the Spanish guy was rubbing his genitals against her small round behind. From time to time, she would bend forward and the Spanish guy would mount her, simulating the sexual act. Throughout the dance an innocent dreamy expression never left the girl's face. I was observing a ritual dance, eons old.

Watching the performance, the crowd got hot. There were the dozens of disheveled young women who much earlier left the confinement of their offices and now made a B-line for the dance floor. Hot with a thirst that couldn't be quenched by the city born and bred of feeble manhood, unable to express their impatience and tension through dancing for lack of space, they climbed onto the stage – the only place that could allow some movement – and went wild. More and more women climbed on. Finally, there were so many of them – they started dropping off the stage like overripe fruit.

While all around me people were singing and swaying to the music. Being unable to share their joy, their experience of oneness with the music and with each other, I was overcome by a taunting sadness. All I was aware of was the deafening noise, cigarette smoke eating at my eyes and the dangerous lack of space. Maybe if I had stayed there a little longer, it would have come to me and I would have experienced this oneness the way a deaf person experiences music, and the blind experiences, colors but we got up to leave. I turned around. The hot sweaty crowd was packed so tightly that in order to survive it had to breathe in unison. The people were unable to move, except for their raised arms waiving to the music. Lit by the bright multi-colored floodlights, the dance floor with the arms waving over it looked like a monstrous sea anemone with its hundred stems swaying in the ocean water. The violet smoke from hundreds of cigarettes rose above the crowd making the whole place look like a gigantic simmering broth.

The door behind me closed with a bang and I hungrily gulped the winter air. Now already early in the morning, the air was free from car exhaust fumes and for a moment sweet and crisp. Snowflakes slowly circled around us in a mysterious drunken dance. The morning silence of the big city enveloped me. It was three o'clock on Sunday morning.

IN THE CITY OF BIG DREAMS

Pale flat chested women in heavy boots
trod the dirty streets of the metropolis
past the stalls exploding with tropical flowers
past the garbage bins
where cats and bag ladies compete for food
past ethnic restaurants
spreading sinful exotic smells down the block,
past the street musician playing a banjo
past drug addicts sprawled on the pavement
past lovers making out on the corner
to the sounds of the banjo
past shop windows displaying ephemeral bridal gowns,
their eyes firmly fixed on the ground
never expecting and never expected,
never giving and never taking.
Hurt has blinded them,
and locked their hearts
and thrown the keys away.
Thus they keep walking through life,
their feet shod in heavy boots
their eyes firmly fixed on the ground
their long lovely hair tortured in a bun
unloved and unloving
unforgiven and unforgiving,
their color and smile
sapped by the endless fight for survival
in the city of big dreams.
From my window they look like spacewomen,

and if you take away their heavy boots,
their anorexic bodies
will lift and float away.
"But why survive at all?" I ask.
They won't disclose that to anyone
not even to a poet.

THE REFLECTIONS OF AN IMMIGRANT

Mastering the Art of Sharing

Why, why, why do these characters take a liking to me? You know, those types, who go to holistic places, who are always in search of the right partner, always going through some type of crisis or other and are collecting everybody's opinion as to what they should do about it, only to do nothing in the end, which is exactly what they will do anyway, every time?

The last time Bruce and I went to this Himalayan yoga retreat there was a woman there whose facial expression suggested utter displeasure. She looked as if she had bitten on something sour, and was just waiting for the right moment to spit it out. Sitting six feet away from her table in the dining hall, I observed how kind and attentive everyone was to her, but the sour expression never left her face. I knew it was only the matter of time before she discovered my existence.

It happened when she snuck up on Bruce and me as we were walking down a hidden path in the woods and interrupted the idyllic rustling of the leaves with her high-pitched voice, "Oh, I had no idea there was a path here." That's when I sat down on the trunk of a fallen tree and refused to move even one inch beyond that point. So did she. After a few moments of polite conversation during which we sized each other up and concluded that neither of us was going to budge, I explained to her where the path was leading and then excused myself by saying that we had decided to go the other way. Afterwards, Bruce delivered a lengthy lecture on how rude it was of me to behave this way and that I should learn to share myself with others less fortunate.

Totally ashamed of myself, I decided to make every conscious effort to eradicate this selfish trait of my character.

The opportunity presented itself when I accepted a long put-off invitation of my former high school teacher Anna. Frankly speaking, paying visits to my high school teachers is not my favorite pastime. To make it worse, lately Anna's invitations have become more persistent which has led me to believe that she was about to ask me for a favor, and for some mysterious reason was reluctant to do so on the phone. This had only further dampened my spirit. But in view of my previously made decision, on a gloomy March morning, I set out to share myself selflessly with her and her husband Alex.

My visit starts with a tour of the kitchen where Alex proudly displays all the things that strange Americans throw out. There is a TV set, a cordless iron, a couple of books in the language that he doesn't understand, a multitude of frame less pictures, picture less frames and a hand less clock. Each object's demonstration is followed by a detailed account of the circumstances under which it has been rescued and description of all replaced parts as well as an estimate of what else could be done to improve its appearance and usefulness. In Latvia Alex was a nuclear scientist. His garbage expeditions, archaeological in nature, became an outlet to his creativity.

Alex and Anna were in their late fifties when they followed their two children Mila and Pyotr to America. By the time they reached the United States, their children who had left Latvia two years prior to their parents' arrival had bitterly quarreled and settled down on the opposite areas of the one of the largest cities on the planet Earth – New York. Consequently, Anna and Alex often found themselves without the much needed help of their children, and that's where I came in handy. I helped them with the numerous forms and applications that they had to fill out, the plethora of papers they received from various agencies and telephone calls that had to be made to various institutions.

Now that they have finally settled down in Bay Ridge, Alex has found himself a job cleaning Suzy Chen's offices for five dollars an hour. He does so off the books for both he and Anna are on welfare. Suzy Chen specializes in helping people lose weight. She came up with a line of prepackaged and frozen food that is sold to thousands of overweight clients. As a Suzy Chen's employee, Alex gets to take home all the damaged cans as well as the packages of frozen dishes that are nearing their expiration date. Today I've been invited over to partake of Suzy Chen's dinner.

I am sitting on the sofa in their living room where Anna is engaging me in polite conversation. Meantime, strange sounds are emanating from the kitchen where Alex is engaged in dinner preparation. We hear cursing, objects falling down, the stomping of his feet and the sound of running water. It's clear that much more is going on in the kitchen than the mere warming up of food. Much to my surprise, Anna exhibits no anxiety over the sounds coming from the kitchen, which leads me to believe that they are a part of their everyday existence. Well, I'm wrong. Suddenly Alex appears in the doorway and announces that the kitchen is on fire. We run out of the room and get the glimpse of Alex plunging into the clouds of smoke. The kitchen appears to be a volcano at the height of eruption. Sometimes we get a glimpse of his arm or foot in a brown felt slipper, but the rest of him is immersed in the clouds of black smoke. "What's burning?" Anna shouts. Out of the clouds comes his desperately calm voice "I have no idea." And then, "Open the front door." We unlock the door and release smoke into the staircase. Anna seems to be disoriented. First, she starts running down the steps, then stops, turns around and runs back into the apartment, where she again stops hesitantly in the doorway.

Meantime, the source of fire has been discovered. The culprits are Alex's tools of trade – all those sponges, rags and brushes he uses to clean Suzy Chen's offices. He thought he had put them out of the way by hiding them under the stove, but when he started warming up the frozen trays of Suzy Chen's dinner in the oven, they caught on fire. Now that the fire is finally out, Alex is cleaning the kitchen, which is covered with the thick carpet of soot. We with Anna are back on the sofa in the living room where she is telling me about the urgent plea of her oldest grandson Pyotr.

Pyotr is a student at The New York City Tech. He is on welfare. According to welfare regulations he is supposed to be living on his own. Yet, in fact, he continues living with his parents. This important fact has to be concealed from the welfare department. That is why Anna asks me to write a letter stating that he is presently residing with me. Just as I am about to voice my feeble protest, she picks up the phone and calls Pyotr to find out how exactly the letter should be worded. Pyotr says that it has to state that from me, he rents a room.

There is a knock on the door. It's the super asking if the apartment is on fire. Alex calls me into the corridor to translate. I interrupt my conversation with Pyotr and explain to the super what has just transpired. The latter is shaking his head incredulously but in the end seems to be satisfied with my explanation. When he leaves, my conversation with Pyotr is interrupted again, this time by a knock on the door from a concerned neighbor asking if everything is all right. I don't wait for an invitation from Alex when I hear another loud and urgent knock on the door. I open the door. It is a fireman. I've never seen a fireman so close. He looks enormous in his gear, filling up the whole anteroom and reminds me of a medieval knight.

"You called the fire brigade?" he asks.

"No, we didn't."

"Do you know who did?"

"I have no idea."

The moment the door closes behind the fireman, Alex flies into the room as if ricocheted out of the kitchen. "Tell him, tell the fireman," he is screaming while still in orbit, that we didn't call them. "Tell him or they will send a bill!" "I've already told him so," I try to calm him down, " anyway, firemen here don't send bills."

The phone is ringing. It is Pyotr. He wants the letter to be worded differently. He has just spoken to a friend of his who has warned him that should the letter state that he is renting a room from me, they might ask him for a lease at the welfare office. It would therefore be better if I wrote that we are sharing the apartment. However, it must be specified that we take our meals separately.

While I am jotting down this pertinent piece of information, Anna is cleaning the kitchen from soot. Alex is trying to light a pilot light in the oven, which got extinguished when he poured water over the fire. When he fails to do so, he departs to get the super. They both come into the kitchen. "Tell him, that I am unable to light the pilot light in the oven," says Alex. I translate. "Tell him that I am not authorized to do this work," replies the super. "An appointment has to be made with the gas company." Seeing Alex's surprise, he plunges into a lengthy description of his duties as a super. Being himself a recent immigrant from Yugoslavia he does so in broken English. He points to the walls, the floor and the ceiling and explains that he takes care of these, but he doesn't take care of the gas stove, which is the responsibility of the gas company. "If you make an appointment now, how long do we have to wait?" asks Alex. "A week," replies the super. "What? A week? You mean the gas will be leaking the whole week?" Alex's voice climbs into the upper register. "He can't help it," I explain on behalf of the super. The super departs with the intention of making an appointment with the gas company. While Alex loudly bewails his destiny, I silently bewail mine, for it doesn't seem like I'll be getting out of here any time soon. Resigned to my fate I return to the living room. Alex reappears. Now he wants to know the English equivalent of " Ya vsyo ispravil." "I've fixed it." I translate. "I fix it, I fix it," he repeats triumphantly. "This lazy bum just didn't want to get his hands dirty." He departs to inform the super that the appointment with the gas company is no longer necessary for the pilot light is finally on.

Ana and I set the table in the living room. Alex is back stuffing the oven with Suzy Chen's trays of frozen food. He takes a pot and starts making soup. He empties the content of several packages into a pot and pours water over it. The plates I am putting on the table are covered with soot but I am not going to say one word about it. I want to get this meal over and done with as quickly as possible, even if I have to eat out of dirty dishes.

When we finally sit down to eat, Ana is still feebly trying to play a hostess, while Alex is sitting at the table listlessly. Not a word escapes his lips until it's time for the second course. It is then that he notices that a fork is missing from his set of silverware. "Of course, everyone has a fork, but do I have a fork?" he raises his voice dramatically, "No, I don't have a fork," and continues sitting there as if cast in stone. Ana runs into the kitchen to get him a fork. The second course tastes like the version of the same bland soup only in a crystallized form and is characterized by an identical lack of taste. We get a dessert, which tastes much like the second course only coated with sweet milk chocolate.

Alex says he is feeling tired, excuses himself and lies down on the sofa in the living room. Ana suggests the two of us go for a walk. We go out. It is cold. In the gray sky the wind is tearing clouds apart like an angry dog. The smell of the recent fire follows me everywhere we go; I realize that I am getting sick. In about forty minutes we return home and I get ready to leave. Alex offers to see me to the bus stop. I obstinately refuse. Exhausted by the day's events he doesn't press the issue. They stuff my backpack with cans of Suzy Chen's diet food. Too weak to protest I take my backpack and depart. It's a long way to the bus stop. I run. I crawl. With every step my nausea is increasing. It's growing, expanding, assuming strange shapes and manifestations. Smells, sounds and colors are magnified tenfold. It is starting to snow. On this late Sunday afternoon the streets are deserted; not even a stray cat crosses my road. When I finally reach the bus stop, I wait for the bus for a long time peering into the cold starless night. The wind is so strong and I am feeling so weak that had it not been for the backpack filled with the cans of diet food I'd be rolling up and down Thirteenth Avenue like an empty soda can.

By the time I reach home I have the most horrible case of food poisoning. I make it to the bathroom and from there to the bedroom where I faint on the bed. I come to only to discover to my total humiliation that diarrhea has overcome me. I get into the shower and then stuff the soiled sheets into the laundry bag. As I am doing so, I hear the key turning in the door. The door opens and there is Bruce standing in the doorway. "Hi, honey," he says in a slightly sheepish tone, which he assumes when business keeps him away from home on the weekend. "What have you been doing with yourself today?" I turn to him, a bag of soiled sheets in hand and say gloomily, "I've been sharing myself selflessly, dear."

THE CASE OF THE ADJUSTABLE BED

Bruce and I were married last December. I thought that in the three years I had known the man prior to this event, I got to know him pretty well. Yet as soon as we exchanged our yes-I do's, he started dishing out one surprise after another. The latest surprise came as an adjustable bed, the one that gets up when you get up and lies down when you do. You see it advertised on TV a lot.

One afternoon Bruce came home and informed me rather matter-of-factly that he had invited a salesman over to tell us about an adjustable bed. Now thinking all the way back I remember the adventurous gleam in his eyes that should have warned me right then that it wasn't a simple matter. But as an inexperienced newlywed whose attention was totally absorbed by a soup preparation, I carelessly ignored what I later learned to recognize as a sign of pending trouble, the sign that would immediately send me to enlist the help of my family, friends, and depending on its intensity, even the National Guard. That time though I replied sweetly that I was in no way interested in an adjustable bed. All I wanted was a bedroom set that consisted of a bed, a dresser and a wardrobe, and if for some reason he still wanted to see the salesman, he was free to do so, but he would have to count me out. "Okay, okay," grumbled Bruce as he sat down at the table to eat his dinner. Our minds being occupied with an upcoming trip to Florida, this conversation had completely evaporated out of mind until one day when Bruce came home from work with a terrible migraine headache. He sat down at the table looking like a sick bird, his head hanging on the left side (the sight that used to arouse my compassion). All of a sudden there came a loud cheerful voice from the intercom announcing that there was a Mr. Hinley to talk to us about an adjustable bed. All the pity I felt for my sickly husband sank in a roaring sea of irritation. Having left my dinner on the table, I hastily retreated to apartment 6-B where Mrs. Warretsky resided. There I spent hours listening to her complaints about her demanding boss, her crippling arthritis and ungrateful children. I could hear excited voices coming from our apartment that was located over a court yard exactly opposite Mrs. Warretsky's. "Well, at least one of us is having fun," I thought gloomily. Three hours later Bruce appeared in the window and announced that the salesman was gone and I could return home.

When I opened the door I saw Bruce's happy face..

"I bought it," he said.

"You what?"

"I bought the bed."

"How much?"

"A couple thousand dollars."

So it was. The man had bought the bed. Are you sitting or standing? If you are standing , sit down. If you are sitting, lie down. If you are lying down, there is nothing left for you, but to die. He bought it for one fourth of his yearly income. I wonder how he manages to suffer from those migraine headaches. The man has no head! When I tried to find out what made him do it, he told me that it was a combination of his migraine headache and the salesman's foul breath that drove him to this desperate act. Yet one look at him would tell you a different story. The man was craving the bed. As I gently but firmly voiced my opinion against the purchase, he started looking more and more like a bird that was all set to fly to a warm country, only to find out that its wings had been clipped, and that there was no way it could get off the ground. Tears came down his cheeks. Between sighs and sobs he managed to tell me the story of a beautiful adjustable bed that comes with a fifteen-year guarantee and is used in every hospital in the country, the bed that gives you a healthy back, healthy look, adds ten years to your life, plus that special touch to your marriage. He also said that I would have never felt the way I did about the adjustable bed, had I heard the salesman's presentation and smelled his foul breath. It took me a couple of hours to calm him down. In the end I prevailed and Bruce promised to cancel the purchase. But the thought still haunts me.

What if his desire for the bed was too strong for him to resist? What if he said that he was going to cancel the order but never did it? Each time I hear the intercom, panic seizes me. What if it is the bed being delivered, then what do I do? The brochures left by the salesman on the table, titled "Heavenly Sleep," "Your Healthy Back," depicting on their covers gray haired folks in pajamas lying in an adjustable bed, smiling at each other in a warm understanding fashion. A big hideous sign "I Sleep In An Adjustable Bed" is the indelible reminder of this event. Well, marriage is no laughing matter.

THE CHAIR

Once upon a time there was a chair, an old wooden chair that Bruce brought home from his mother's house in Philadelphia several years ago. It was made of cherry wood with an elegantly tilted back for the comfort of the person sitting in it. Its seat was made of a nice beige woven fabric that became faded with time. It also had three planks under the seat – two in the back and one in the front for sturdiness.

The chair lived in the bedroom of Bruce and his wife Irina. It was a nice spacious bedroom with a king sized bed. To the right of the chair there was a table, also made of cherry wood, to the left and a little above it on the wall there was a reproduction of Picasso's painting which depicted a face of a young woman with a pair of big dreamy eyes entangled in the jungle of long curly unruly hair. The chair used to chat with the beautiful young lady, but avoided socializing with the table that had a lap top siting on top of it for the chair happened to have a genuine dislike for lap tops.

In Bruce's and Irina's home the chair lived a calm and peaceful life, but it had one major problem. They were always hanging their clothes on it. Irina's skirt, Bruce's pants and sometimes even a towel would land on it. The chair got very tired of it. You see, it wanted to be a chair, but nobody would sit on it anymore because of all the clothes hanging on it. It couldn't even display its proudly tilted back because it was always covered by one of Irina's long fashionable skirts. And when the chair would talk to the young lady with dreamy eyes in the picture its voice coming from underneath the clothes sounded muffled which was very embarrasing.

So one day it got so fed up that it decided to fight back and when Irina hung her red t-shirt on it,the chair threw it right back at her. And then Bruce's pants, a pair of his new stripped socks, his underwear, and Irina's newly purchased skirt from Macy's – all went flying through the air. For you see, the chair wanted to be sat in and loved. That's how Irina and Bruce learned to respect its constitutional rights and they never hung clothes on it again. From then on they always hung them in the closet instead.

This is the happy ending of the chair story.

INSTRUCTIONS FOR BRUCE

Bruce is a middle-aged 6'5, 206 lb, black hair, green eye Caucasian male with a mole on his left cheek whose possession I assumed twenty-two years ago. Regrettably, he came without a manual, which would have made my life much easier. It's taken me two decades of hard work and experimentation to come up with a set of instructions. I feel it to be my obligation to save my successor (should there be one) from the harrowing experience I have been through. Therefore, with no small amount of foresight, I have firmly requested that Bruce should keep this document in his possession at all times.

Please, read the following instructions carefully before operating this homo sapien, it may save your life.

How B-R-U-C-E Works

Prior to calling his name, cough, sneeze or shuffle your feet to alert him to your existence and the possibility of interaction. Then gently call out his name, "Bruce." Allow him a minimum of six seconds to stabilize and repeat his name, "Bruce." This time it is advisable to put a bit of urgency into your voice. The switch will click, the light will go on and Bruce will start downloading.

She says, "Bruce."

Who is Bruce?

She is looking straight at me. Is it me?

Yes, I am Bruce.

Where am I?

The list of possible locations appears: Mars, Venus, Jupiter, Earth.
I am on planet Earth.
What century is it?
XXI century.
What year?
2016.
Here Bruce's mind usually takes a poetic detour.
Wow! It is the XXI century. Pyramids, Edward Casey, Pharaoh, extraterrestrials…

At this point on the screen of a computer you would read, "W-A-I-T", which communicates to you that it cannot accept any further command until it has digested the previous one. Unlike a computer that has been designed to get over this difficulty on his own, Bruce hasn't. Therefore, you may have to repeat his name several times to ensure that he is online. "Bruce, Bruce, Bru-u-uce."

Yes, I am Bruce.
This command is for me.
What does she want?
An umbrella?
What's an umbrella?
A device that protects one from rain.
Where is it?
She is pointing right behind me.
It must be here, in the corner, behind the shelf.
Is this it?
She keeps repeating, " The blue one. The blue one."
What is blue?
We keep fighting over colors.
What she says is blue, I know is green.
O-o-oh! She is getting annoyed! Trouble!
Grab one. Any one. Show it to her. Raise your eyebrows.
She is nodding.
You've got it right!
After you have familiarized yourself with these proceedings, please read the following chapter.
Warning

Do not exceed one command at a time to avoid an overload. Bruce will accept only one command at a time. Should you opt to make some changes in your command, make your command audible and check if Bruce is on line. Remember that your new instructions will not automatically void the previous one. Bruce experiences tremendous difficulty registering changes.

In case a prompt reaction is required, it is helpful to exhibit your utmost agitation prior to giving a command. For example, "A-a-a-ah! Turn it off! The red pot! Right behind you! No, the one behind it. Yes, that's the one." Always acknowledge the properly carried out command.

It doesn't matter how hard you try to give him the most detailed instructions. For example, "Bruce. Please. My bag. On the other side of the counter." (Note the short incomplete sentences I use to avoid the overload.) To supplement my instructions, I also point to the object with my hand. You would think that at times he would locate the right object by mistake. Abandon all hope. It is not going to happen. I've tried to make the following suggestion, "Bruce, visualize what you are going to do next and do exactly the opposite." It didn't help either.

Two weeks ago we were shopping in Brighton. I went into a store and Bruce stayed outside, about thirty feet away, guarding numerous packages. While waiting on line I approximated how much money I will need to pay for the purchases. It looked like I was short of cash. There were still a few people in front of me, so I poked my head out of the door, waved to Bruce and shouted, "Come closer, Bruce. I may need some cash." When I came to the register it appeared that I was right. I was $3 short. Again I poked my head out of the door anticipating to see Bruce outside. No way, Bruce was standing in his previous position thirty feet away from the store. I hollered for him to come over and we paid for the purchases under the disapproving stares of other customers waiting in line. Once outside the store I asked Bruce if he had seen me open the door and look for him. "Well, I did see you open the door and look for somebody," he admitted hesitantly, "but I wasn't sure who you were looking for."

Yesterday we went out for a cup of coffee. I liked the song they were playing in the café and asked Bruce if he knew where the song was from. "From the radio," answered Bruce quite annoyed at my stupidity.

For some reason beyond my understanding Bruce appears to be determined to self-destruct himself with work but he always comes down with a flu when he is half way there. That's when I nurse him back to health. When he finally gets out of bed and stumbles into the kitchen on a pair of long thin shaky legs, he reminds me of a baby giraffe who is trying to figure out how to use his extremities for the first time, as if they were a pair of stilts. "How are you feeling?" I ask him, my voice warm with compassion. "Well," he says. "I do feel better, but I am still not a hundred percent." "You were born ninety percent." I tell him. "How can you expect to be a hundred percent after a flu?" "Well," he says, "my temperature is normal, so I was thinking…" "Make no mistake," I say, "the temperature is the only thing that's normal about you."

Sometimes when I get frustrated, I ask, "Bruce, how did they make you?" He shrugs his shoulders. "I guess, the same way they made everyone else. You see," he confesses, "I was supposed to come back as an animal but at the last moment there was an opening in the human department and I was upgraded to human status."

Since no in vitro fertilization existed at the time of his conception, I guess, I can't blame it on science. Neither can I sue the man upstairs. But in times of utter frustration I call out to God, "God, do you see this? I know that you cannot do anything about it, but do you at least see this? Please, give me a sign." I've never received any answer and neither will you. All you can do at this point is to follow my instructions carefully. Should you notice any changes that occur in Bruce, kindly record them in the manual. Good luck and G-d's speed.

ONE WOMAN'S MORNING

It's six o'clock on a dark winter morning. Dreams are still on my eyelashes. I am getting out of the bed and shuffling my way into the kitchen. I fix a kettle of water and take my medication. I remind myself to first let the water run, because in old houses like ours the pipes are rusty and so is the water that runs through them. Then, I pour the water into a Brita filter and watch it slowly seep through. Done. The old teapot is murmuring reassuringly. I open the fridge and realize that last night I had forgotten to pick up a loaf of bread on my way home. Then, to my relief I notice some slices through a plastic bag tucked in the corner of the bottom shelf. Lucky me! There are four of them exactly, so there is Bruce's lunch.

The weather forecast is next. I tape it every morning for my English as a Second Language students. I turn on the radio. "Breakfast with Bill and Barbara." Now I'll have to wait until they cheerfully announce the weather forecast. I hate Barb's pseudo-intellectual sexy voice. She kind of drags it, in the hope that if her words take more space, they'll also carry more weight. For some reason this is the only voice that my students understand.

The teapot is whistling. Where is my pill? What time is it? 6:55. Half an hour before breakfast after having my Tibetan medication with hot water. I can have my cup of tea at 7:25. Note 7:25. Where is the darn weather forecast? Enough about murder and cataclysms. I know that we are nearing the very end. But before everything ends, I've got to tape my weather forecast. Lunch for Bruce. One sandwich with cheese. Not too much mayonnaise. "I am not particularly fond of mayonnaise, Irene." Another one with peanut butter and jelly. Wrap'em up. An apple. Bruce stumbles into the kitchen. Eyes half closed. A hug and a kiss.

"Good morning, honey. Do we have a new tube of toothpaste? The old one is finished."

"Yes, we do."

"Where?"

"On the second shelf."

"Where on the second shelf?"

"In the corner."

"I don't see it."

"Here it is."

Darn it. I've missed it. "Tomorrow cloudy, windy with drizzle in the morning...." And what about today?

Wheateana is boiling. Lower the fire. Add raisins, butter and milk. Milk? There is no milk. I open a can of condensed milk instead. Let's hope he doesn't notice the difference. Gosh! It's 7:30. I'd better get dressed.

"We'll have the weather forecast after the Bowary Minute." If I don't turn the tape recorder on now I may miss it again, for you never know how long the Bowary Minute may last. Bruce standing in the doorway accusingly: "You haven't fixed my pants." "Sorry. I had no time last night. Tonight. I'll fix it tonight. I promise! I swear! Honest!" Deep, mournful sigh escapes his lungs. Where did I hear this before? Sea lions at the Brighton aquarium.

"I depart today. This is my last announcement," a Zen master wrote on 60 postcards on the day of his death. To think that one can depart in such good health. Think how much energy you need to write this on 60 postcards, plus your address and signature? I wonder if he also wrote the sender's address on them. But then, it makes no sense to write the sender's address when you are going to depart, does it?

It's 7:40. Now ten minutes for acupuncture. Who has 10 minutes for anything? My friend Janet says that if you don't have 10 minutes for acupuncture in the morning – life is not worth living.

And who said it is? Certainly not me. Ouch, it hurts, especially the top of my ear. Two minutes, two and a half....... three.......

"Honey, what tie should I wear?"

Here he is standing before me, wearing a grey suit and a green shirt and asking me what tie he should wear. Yellow, of course. It's 7:50 by the kitchen clock.

"Take another shirt"

"Which one?"

"The white one."

"I have no clean shirts left. They are all in the laundry."

"Of course, you have. . . In the first closet. Here it is."

Oh, no! I forgot to turn the tape recorder off. How on earth will I be able to find the weather forecast now? Relax. Play it back. Plants. Two in the bedroom should be sprayed, two in the living room watered. The plant over the sofa starts dripping, of course. Put a rag under it.

Here is the weather forecast at last. Now I've got to transcribe it.

"Bruce, how do you spell Massachusetts?'

He gives me the spelling.

"Bye, honey. Call me at work, will you?"

"Of course I will."

There is a run in my pantyhose. And it is only the second time that I've worn them. It is 8:20.

If I leave now I'll be O.K. I remind myself to take the tape out of the tape recorder. So many times have I run out without it.

Oh, Lord, please not this. Not this time. I swear this is too much. WHERE ARE MY KEYS?

Not on the dresser, not on the table, not in the corridor..... Oh, here they are. . . Thank you, Lord, thank you, thank you. . .

"What was the article about that I was reading over somebody's shoulder on the subway last night?" I ask myself as I am running down the steps, which is certainly quicker than waiting for the elevator. It said women are not romantic anymore. It said that they have lost their romanticism. Lost it, my foot! They've been robbed of it at gunpoint, I say to myself as I open the door. The time is 8:35.

TIRED WIFE'S BLUES

Yes, I have learned to live without hope,
Sleep without dreams,
Work without giving it much thought,
Smile flashing my dental work
Rather than my eyes
And consume food without calories
And drinks without sugar.
But have you ever noticed I am dead?
It is my corpse that serves you dinner every night
And smiles at you when you wake up on Sunday morning.
I dress it well
So it would look attractive and I perfume it
So it wouldn't stink.
And people tell me that it looks quite lovely.
But
Has anybody ever noticed I am dead?

THE OTHER SIDE OF THE WALL

"In America smart people do not take themselves too seriously."

Nina Berberova

When Elena and Pavel came to New York in August it was so hot that they could sleep under the wet sheets only. The mother and son settled down in Brooklyn and were introduced to us by my sister Natasha during her visit to the Big Apple in the hope that Bruce and I would be of some assistance to them. Since then Elena and Pavel have often called us asking for help with translation, storage space for their work, money and papers. Elena usually made the calls. "It's Ele-e-na-a," she would start in a low plaintive drone-like voice and my husband Bruce would hastily drop the receiver in my hand as if it were a hot potato. "It's Natasha's revenge calling," he would whisper, alluding to my less than perfect relationship with my sister Natalie and hastily relocate into the bedroom. On those rare occasions when Pavel ventured to make a call himself, he would always start with, "Hello, this is Pavel. It's nice to see your voice."

Both Pavel and his mother were photographers by trade; Pavel also painted. In Latvia they had a couple of exhibitions and won some prizes. They felt that in the Soviet block their freedom of expression was limited and expected to get some attention upon their arrival in the US. To their total dismay they found that in the country of the free nobody had ever heard of them, seen their artwork or cared to see it. Having no work permit, they could not get a job or afford an apartment. For a while they shared their living quarters with a family of five Soviet emigres and existed on Elena's meager earnings as a cleaning lady. However, even a cleaning job was hard to get, for Elena bore a stamp of such anguish that people felt uncomfortable hiring her. Her pale face, framed in short dark hair with deep mournful creases running down her cheeks, looked as if it had stayed pressed between the pages of an old heavy volume for some time. On such a terrain a smile was not only alien, it was inappropriate. In order to get a job in America you've got to smile or at least be capable of it. Elena was in her late fifties, small, thin but not fragile. Her wardrobe consisted of a skirt, two tops and a red woolen jacket. Pavel who was in his late twenties, having been shielded from life by his mother did not set into his own mold yet. The young man was nondescript and pale as if he had just crawled out from underneath a rock. He wore heavily framed tortoise shell glasses.

Things became easier as they entered into an arrangement where they were given a room in return for taking care of an old sick Russian woman. Then another break came. After years of trying to obtain a legal status, Pavel won a green card lottery and was now about to become a law-abiding emigre. There was one obstacle though. He had to pay a big fine for having stayed in the US illegally. That's when they called us asking for a loan and we agreed to help them.

A couple of days later I called to let them know that we were on our way. As I was speaking to Pavel I heard screams and commotion in the background. "What's going on?' I asked. "We are getting ready for your arrival," he said. "Mom is washing the old bitch who is putting up a fight."

We searched for the address written on the card given to us by Pavel. They lived in a bad neighborhood and I felt apprehensive about going there with a lot of cash. Bringing them a check was out of question for they had no bank account. We came to a big old redbrick apartment building on Ocean Avenue and walked to the elevator. When its door opened it let out a burly black fellow with a menacing face. I was ready to sink on my knees and hand him the bundle of cash stuffed in my left coat pocket, but he passed without as much as giving us a glance, leaving a trail of a cheap shaving lotion aroma behind. On the fifth floor we got out and rang the bell. Nina let us in and we followed her into the living room where an old woman with a hard hostile face, was lying on a couch in front of a big screen blaring TV watching a program about orangutans. The woman did not respond to our hello. There was a sickening sweet smell in the air. The window was wide open and the room was clean.

Elena led us into a small room with a door that would not close. The walls were painted the bright color of cheap raspberry ice cream. An enormous armorer with a mirror took half of the room. A small table, a chair and a queen-sized bed that Elena and her son shared, filled the rest of the space. Pavel's only pair of boots given to him a year ago by my sister was drying on the windowsill. He suggested that I should sit down on the bed. Bruce was offered the only chair in the room. I asked if I could sit down in the chair instead. "We can try this arrangement if you wish," Pavel said hesitantly, looking at my big frame," but the chair is not too sturdy". After that I cautiously landed on the bed, which gave a painful resigned squeak.

The old woman was not as sick as she pretended to be, they explained. When they were at home, she would lie in bed moaning loudly and persistently but when she found herself alone, she would get up and walk around the apartment. They figured that out after it was discovered that certain objects had a tendency to move during their rare absences. She would not ask for a bedpan but relieve herself right in bed and Nina had to change the sheets and wash her again and again. They told us that the old woman's daughter was a drunk and a drug addict who lived in the apartment below. She milked her mother for the little money that was left from her Social Security checks. The daughter was constantly checking if Elena and Pavel were home, because according to the agreement one of them had to be in the apartment at all times. Since officially only Elena was supposed to be living there, Pavel had to hide in the closet each time a social worker made a visit to the apartment. He was terrified of the old woman and when his mother was away would not even step out of the room to make himself a cup of tea.

Pavel took out some photographs stacked behind the bed and showed us their artwork. I was surprised to see an image of a brick wall in some of them. "Oh, you'll see a wall in many of our pictures," said Pavel. "As you know yourself, Irina, in Soviet Latvia the rest of the world was closed to us. We were not allowed to cross the borders of the Soviet Union, read foreign press or listen to foreign radio stations. We were burning with desire to climb over and see what was on the other side. And now we are on the other side. There is no grass here. It's not that it has been cut; it's been burned out by poison. Graffiti is painted all over the wall and a drug addict is sprawled in the pool of his own vomit under it." Looking through the pictures I was struck by the feeling of heavenly depth and astral mystery that reminded me of Tarkovsky's movies. Elena told us that in her youth she was dreaming of becoming an astronomer and spent nights watching stars on the roof. Pavel brought us more pictures. The space being handled similarly in both Elena's and Pavel's photographs, it was often difficult to tell their work apart. The unusual thing about Pavel's photographs was that they bore little resemblance to the actual subject matter. It's as if the artist in him had rebelled against the main purpose of photography, which is to give as precise image of an object as possible. Instead, he would present an object at an angle, which would take it out of its context, startle the viewer, catch him unawares and make him search for the meaning of the photograph. He showed us several photographs of my niece, Anat who was ten years old at the time the pictures were taken. Dressed in a long over sized raincoat, with her features slightly dimmed, she bore a look of a twenty year old woman. In another picture she was holding a tin can on her head. The photograph made it appear as a crown and was called "Queen Sheba". Pavel has also shown us some of his paintings. Contrary to his photographs, the objects in his paintings didn't have enough space . They looked as if they were trying to break the frame and get out of their confined space.

Throughout our conversation Elena was persistently referring to her son as Michelangelo. She told us about a famous clairvoyant in Riga who had predicted that after enduring eight years of tremendous hardship her son was to become the most famous artist of his time. Even though there was not enough money for food, they were reluctant to part with his paintings. "Why sell?" said Elena. "He will never paint like this again. His next picture will be quite different."

She took my hand and placed it on her ribs, so that I could feel how thin she became. "We both lost 15 pounds each in the first month of being in the US," she said. "I am constantly hungry and we have only twelve dollars left."

During our conversation the phone rang several times, but when Elena answered it, no one was there. "It's her daughter checking up on us," explained Elena. The next time the phone rang the daughter responded and Elena complained to her about the mice in the building. She said that she had put several mousetraps in the apartment and each of them caught a mouse.

On the other side of the wall we could hear the sounds of gunshots and bloodcurdling screams coming from the Western on TV, which could not drown the old woman's persistent demanding moans. "She wants attention," explained Elena, but remained sitting.

They insisted that we should accept one of Pavel's paintings as collateral. It was a portrait of Nina depicted with one cloud on top of her head and another one entering through one ear and leaving through the other. "It's worth $3000 or maybe more," Nina said proudly and beamed at us.

We passed the old woman again on the way out of the apartment. She was lying on the sofa naked from the waist down, her blanket on the floor. "Don't look at her," said Elena to us. "Behave yourself or they'll take you away!" she shouted to the old woman who in response lit us with the ray of her menacing evil eye.

In the end I found it too difficult to endure the mixture of grandeur and total desperation that Elena and Pavel were communicating. "It helps when you happen to like the people whom you are helping," said Bruce. He had a point. The last time I met Pavel and Elena in Brooklyn they were working as home attendants. They both put on some weight, which looked far better on Pavel than on his mother. Pavel got himself a French beret, a computer and was trying to promote their artwork on the Internet.

JEFF

My hairdresser Jeff lives on the outskirts of New York, in Mill Basin, which is part of Brooklyn. He moved there from Sheepshead Bay half a year ago and now I've got to spend an hour and a half getting there from Boro Park and change three buses in the process. When Bruce tells me that the next day he'll be able to drive me to Mill Basin, I call Jeff to book the first appointment next morning. As we approach Jeff's house the next day, I am always anxious to see if there are any other cars parked in his driveway, which would mean, of course, that he has squeezed in a client or two before me.

Today when we pull up at his house at ten minutes to nine I see two cars parked in his driveway. I open the door and go downstairs into his shop. Jeff is already working full speed. This is the way he works seven days a week, three of them in a Beauty Salon and four at home. He would work the eighth day too had God created eight days in the week. All this hard work has paid off though and last year Jeff, a Turkish immigrant bought a Two story house in one of the most prestigious neighborhoods in Mill Basin. It's a piece of a two story residential middle and upper class - America. That's where he now resides with his wife Jan and his four-year old son Timmy. He has also illegally set up his shop in the basement of his own house.

As I open the door I see that Jeff is in the process of dyeing a woman's hair. The other lady has just had her hair done, and a young girl is waiting for her turn. He must have started at eight or even earlier. Now I am stuck here for two hours and so is Bruce who is waiting for me in the car. Jeff greets me warmly and motions for me to sit down. With a grunt, I settle down in a plush waiting chair and pick up a Vogue magazine. A coffee pot is gurgling, spreading thick aroma. Cold October rain is drumming on the windowpane and Humperdink's smooth seductive voice is pouring out of a radio. I get myself a cup of coffee and sip it slowly, blowing on the hot black liquid.

Jeff's three customers are Russian women who have traveled here all the way from Brighton. Two of them are in their late thirties. One woman has brought her daughter who is preparing for her friend's wedding. The daughter who is about seventeen is a pale, heavy girl, dressed in an oversized T-shirt. She is leafing through a pile of magazines in search of a perfect hairdo. The fourth woman in the room is a manicurist. Her huge body is situated at a tiny table covered with neat rows of nail polish. In front of her rests an enormous Italian hero generously stuffed with cheese and salami, oozing mayonnaise, which she consumes slowly and methodically like a boa constrictor slowly eating a wild boar after it had choked it into an unconscious state. In her thick Hispanic accent she makes a point about drinking eight glasses of water each day, in order to flush her kidneys. That's why she has such clear skin, she explains!! Generally it takes her only fifteen minutes in the morning to put her make up on, but lately, however, she's been plagued by these annoying pimples, she sighs. Her listeners readily nod in understanding.

In the meantime, Jeff has finished with the first customer who gets out of the chair with a satisfied grin on her face. The daughter is next. She shows him a picture of a hairdo she has picked out of a magazine. He nods, puts the magazine on the table. I see a picture of a beautiful brown-eyed human tigress looking out at the jungle of unruly curls. "Waiting to be tamed" the caption reads. Jeff starts washing her hair of which she has plenty. This is going to take a while, I sigh to myself. After applying generous amounts of conditioner, Jeff thoroughly rinses her hair out and tightly wraps a towel around her head. The girl is a crisscross between a slug and jellyfish. Pale, heavy, cold and expressionless she is as far removed from the woman in the picture as a cat is from a tiger or a lizard from a crocodile, a fly from an airplane. Her mother, a lady with a double chin and a girlish hairdo is dressed in a jogging suit which hugs her body tightly. It seems that should she allow herself to take a deep breath the suit will split at the seams and all the stuffing will spill out. They are still on the subject of makeup.

She says, she spends half an hour a day on **make up** application. Her daughter, however, she lowers her voice confidentially, spends three hours on this procedure. All three sigh in awe. Then different brands of makeup are discussed at length and in great detail, Maybelline versus Max Factor, Prescriptives versus L'Oreal, or Channel versus Dior.

In the meantime, Jeff gathers the girl's hair in a neat shiny braid, which he masterfully arranges at the nape of her thick, formidable neck. His movements are balanced, elegant and almost meditative. When he is finished, I catch my breath. I am looking at Katherine the Great reincarnated. The girl sees herself in the mirror, freezes for a moment, then bursts into tears, jumps out of the chair and runs upstairs. Her mother follows her in close step. We can hear the girl's loud laments and her mother's voice trying to calm her down.

Amidst all this commotion Jeff, non-plussed, motions me into the chair. Finally, it's my turn. "If somebody see hairstyle like this," he says pointing at the picture in the magazine, "and then see this beautiful seventeen-year girl," he points in the direction of the staircase from which the cascade of loud wailing continues to pour he says, "I give best hairstyle for her. The hairstyle in picture no good." He says emphatically. "Different hair. Different face. Different everything!" The flustered mother returns downstairs, hastily pays for the hairdo and departs. We hear the angry roar of their car in the driveway.

I look at my watch. It is ten thirty. It's my turn now.

FLOWERS AND TRAGEDIES

Sam is a tall, heavy, balding Slavic giant with a round childish face. Twelve years ago he was sent to America by the communist Yugoslavian government to study weapons. He studied computers instead and earned himself a PhD in this field. After ending his studies he decided to stay in the US lest he should rot in jail for disobeying his government's orders. That's how at the age of forty he ended up in New York with no working papers. There he has gotten a position as a computer consultant in a small non-profit organization and is now working illegally at this thankless job for $10 an hour. He is desperate for work papers but his prospects are bleak. Dan, a friend of his, is trying to introduce him to a Canadian woman by the name of Janet, also a Yugoslavian émigré, in the hope that they may strike a relationship which will eventually lead to a marriage and result in Sam's obtaining Canadian citizenship papers. "They are not as good as American papers," Dan admits,"but in your case they will do."

We are sitting by the open window in the living room of Sam's third floor Brooklyn apartment through which the warm waves of freshly baked bread aroma float in from a Jewish bakery downstairs. Dan is coaching Sam on how to speak to Janet when she calls him. "Speak to her slowly," he says, " 'cause this way you'll have to speak less. When she calls say softly, "How ni-i-ice of you to ca-a-a-all me-e-e." "Say it," he insists. Sam is making an honest effort but sounds more like an English as a Second Language learner than a perspective suitor. He is no Pygmalion. Dan, who is a lady's man, rolls up his eyes in desperation. "Last Friday when I spoke to her about you," he says, "I told her that you have lots of money, but she was not impressed. She said she could earn money herself." "What does she do?" asks surprised Sam. "She is a strip-tease dancer in a night club," answers Dan. "Since she is not interested in money, speak to her about your family instead, for instance, about your uncle from Houston who came to meet you in New York when you arrived in America. "My uncle from Houston? What uncle? I've got no uncles." Sam protests adamantly. "Now you have," says Dan firmly, "a very nice family, very generous, but such a tragedy." "What tragedy?" Sam is alarmed. "His beloved wife of twenty-three years passed away from a stroke last year. Beautiful woman, golden heart. Such a nice family and such a tragedy. Speak about the family, all your uncles and aunts, nieces and nephews and how you send them money. Ni-I-I-ice family but lots of tragedy-I-I-ies. Maybe the broad will take pity on you. But no weird stuff, you understand? No PhDs, no Universities and no UFO's. The highest level anybody in your family has ever reached is a car mechanic. The highest degree you have ever earned is a high school diploma. Talk to her about your job in a flower shop." "Flower shop?" "Yes, flower shop. How you tend the flowers and how many kinds of tulips there are, as well as different kinds of organic fertilizers." "Tulips? I know nothing about tulips!" "Go to the library. Do some research. Interview a gardener. You are a PhD, for goodness sake. And if she asks you about your hobby, tell her that you like working on your car. "I love my ca-a-r. Every weekend I work on my ca-a-ar." And don't forget to ask her about her mother and get her mother's telephone number." "What?!" "Yeah, say to her, "I'd love to speak to your mother. Maybe she knows my uncle from Houston. What is her telephone number? You know, Sam, I have a hunch, they can't wait to marry the broad off. But remember, you've got to proceed slowly, with caution and no weird stuff, only flowers and tragedies."

Sam's had enough. "It's three thirty," he says rubbing his big belly. "It's time for a little something." And we go downstairs to get us a falafel.

ANGELO

His name is Angelo. He is Bruce's barber and a dear human being. I think to develop into one at this time and age constitutes a great accomplishment, since everywhere around us we see a proliferation of a different kind. Once it was scientifically proven that there is no afterlife and that we are mere specks of dust in the wind, our morals have plummeted and we have yet to see them arrive at any station.

I met him after the accident which had damaged his hip. Angelo says the accident has robbed him of his old age. No more can he ride his bike or jump off the diving board in the pool. On the wall of his barber shop there is a picture of him balancing himself on his arms on a diving board. "Then, He would say proudly pointing at his photograph, "I would jump up in the air using the mere strength of my arms and fly into the swimming pool like a bird. Many young men tried it but nobody could do it, not one of them. Now with this artificial hip of mine I can do it no more," he would add sadly and his clients nodded their heads with understanding.

That year would have been much better for him had he not gone to Italy. Before making the trip he called his uncle Luiggi as was his custom. This time Luiggi said, "Don't come, Angelo, stay home." But he went anyway being concerned about his ailing uncle's health. A young girl, his niece, was driving the car. "I told her, don't go Felicia, wait," but she didn't listen and there was a bad accident. Everybody in the car got away with bumps and stitches except for Angelo who had to spend two weeks in the hospital where his hip had to be replaced. Now it was difficult for him to work in his barber shop where he has cut men's hair standing up which has been his profession for forty-five years. In that shop he also grew coffee plants and sold them to his customers for five dollars a piece. One of them, the subject of his love and pride grew tall and strong in the corner of his shop and once even got a write up in a local newspaper which featured a picture of smiling Angelo with scissors in hand and the huge coffee plant in the background. "A Tree Grows in Brooklyn" was written under the photograph.

I saw this tree. It was a strong, happy, much loved tree with healthy glistening leaves. Angelo would always greet it and pat its trunk when he came to work in the morning. If it became too warm in the shop, he would prop the door open so it could breathe. Angelo would bless the plant each time he watered it and the plant would bless him back.

I first met Angelo when Bruce and I came to collect Bruce's beret that Angelo had brought him from his trip to Italy. He had purchased it right before the unfortunate accident, held to it all the way through the car crash and brought it to America after they put him back together in the hospital in Rome. The truth of the matter was that Angelo passionately disliked Bruce's hat that we got him in a Soho store. I agree that the hat wasn't exactly a Channel but what is a guy to do when he has such a big head and it is so cold and windy? Each time Angelo would see Bruce wearing his hat he would erupt into," What is a handsome guy like you doing wearing such a weird hat? Your wife got you this hat? In Soho? She doesn't want other girls looking at you, that is what it's all about. Listen, do me a favor, buy yourself a beret." We did try looking for one, but they don't grow berets Bruce's size in America. He tried dozens of them but they all were too small for him. "I'll bring you one from Italy," Angelo would promise each time he saw Bruce wearing the weird thing. And he held his promise.

When Angelo returned from the trip we came to collect Bruce's beret. Angelo and his wife lived in a tiny house with tiny rooms in Bensonhurst. That house was clearly a member of the family, the way his coffee plant was. The rooms were so immaculate that they reminded me of the rooms in a model house. It was hard to believe that people actually lived there, slept in the beds, used the toilet, took showers in the bathroom, and cooked and ate dinners in the kitchen. With their two children grown up and out of the house, the silent parade of dolls and sports trophies stood at attention in their rooms. The misses was as immaculate as her house, every hair in its place, a freshly ironed

214

dress, flowers in the parlor. I wondered where she was from, from Switzerland she told us. That figures, I thought admiring her house.

Bruce's beret arrived in a sealed plastic bag beautifully wrapped in crispy pink sheets of thin paper. It was a woolen beret with a deep navy blue color lined in a red crispy colored paper and a label inside saying "The Classic Basque" which depicted a breathing fire dragon. Under the label the big red letters read "Dragon" and below it "Waterproof." It also had a black rim that smelled of rich leather. As Bruce put it on Angelo looked at me triumphantly. I had to admit that Bruce did look much better in it than in the hat we had bought him in Soho. When we were leaving Angelo's house in addition to the beret he gave us one of his baby coffee plants. "Here, water it twice a week," Angelo told me handing me the coffee plant.

Last Friday Bruce was sad when he came from Angelo's barber shop for Angelo was retiring. It was his last day of work and he was already packing his things in big carton boxes and taking pictures off the walls. Angelo was also sad for he had failed to find a home for his coffee plant. He called every place in the phone book, even the Brooklyn Botanical Gardens. "I have this beautiful coffee plant in my shop, please come and get it" he said to them. But they said they could not do it. Also, the tree might be diseased, in which case it would infect other plants at the Botanical Gardens. "Diseased? Why diseased?" said Angelo. "It's a healthy plant, hasn't been sick a day in its life. It even got a write up in a local newspaper "A Tree Grows in Brooklyn." "Well," they said reluctantly, "If you bring it over, we'll examine it." "Bring it over? How? I cannot lift it. It's huge. It has taken over my shop. Please do send somebody here to take a look at it." But they said they were short staffed and were unable to do it. "What will you do with it?" asked Bruce. "I'll let it die." Angelo's voice shook. "In my tiny house there is no place for it."

Our coffee plant didn't do that well either. Last summer when we went away for a two week vacation we left it in the bathtub together with three other plants. We placed a bucket full of water in the middle of the bathtub and then tore a rag into long strips that were supposed to bring water from the bucket to the plants and irrigate them. You see, there is nobody here who could take care of our plants when we go away once a year. We rent an apartment in a big apartment house and we don't know our neighbors.

Love thy neighbor. How can you love somebody you don't even know? Our plants actually did quite well, except for the coffee plant. By the end of our vacation it lost most of its leaves. Now it is slowly growing them back, but it has gotten diseased and I see discoloration all over its newly grown leaves. Life in this city is not geared towards growing coffee plants I thought sadly, examining the spots on its leaves.

Now I dare you to find another barber who would develop such a dislike for his customer's hat that he would bring him a beret from his vacation. Angelo, dear human being.

ROBIK'S BIRTHDAY

It is Robik's fiftieth birthday and me and Bruce have been invited to a Russian nightclub in Brighton Beach to celebrate. Bruce, though, refuses the invitation, offers to drive me. My husband, Bruce, finds little tolerance for spending a night among the people whose language he doesn't understand. It's not that my compatriots are rude and don't want to include him in their conversation. At the beginning everybody is on their best behavior and speaks English, but once the first sip of vodka passes their lips, the language of our motherland makes a powerful come back and there is no stopping it.

The party starts at eight. After circling the dark deserted streets of Brighton for quite some time, we finally find the place. I get out of the car and open the heavy squeaky door. The lights are bright and a crystal chandelier is sparkling. The club is swarming with people. I look around and see some familiar faces. Most of us who have gathered here tonight have seen little of each other in the last couple of years. It's been all work, fast paced life and, of course, family obligations, affairs, divorces followed by second marriages and a second set of children. These people are exhausted. Tonight we are glad to re-unite. Everybody is dressed to their teeth in starched shirts, dinner jackets and evening dresses. French perfume floats in the air, diamond earrings sparkle, golden bracelets jingle. "Look at you, old devil. You haven't changed one bit," the deep voice is booming behind me. I turn my head. Like a fish in a net, a short balding fellow disappears in the open arms of a tall heavy-set man. While the shorty emerges from the hug and quickly swims away trying to regain his slightly crushed dignity, the heavy-set man turns to his wife, a stocky lady in a green velvet dress with a low cut decollete and says with a sigh," My-my, Mania, what's happened to Sam? Did you see how thin he's become? All his curly hair is gone." Mania who is deeply immersed in chewing her hors d'oeuvres of pickled herring and smoked salmon, shrugs her shoulders indifferently. I think that should she allow herself a slightly wider range of motion, her white abundant flesh may easily slip out of her decollete like vanilla ice cream out of a waffle cone on a hot summer day. Across the hall I recognize some old acquaintances. In the last five years the couple has dyed their hair, capped their teeth and put on considerable weight. They wave to me and cross the hall. After five minutes of conversation I realize that even though their exterior has undergone some careful renovation, their interior is the same. As always, they are trying to impress me with their latest accomplishments, acquisitions and influential friends. We shake hands and part for the next five years.

Dinner is being served. Everybody sits down at the table. Enormous, elaborately decorated dishes are kept in constant supply. There are roasted ducks and chickens, fried fish, boiled cow tongues, white cheeses in olive oil, caviar sandwiches, marinated mushrooms and seafood salads. I wish the food was as good as the looks of the young waiters in starched shirts in whose strong arms the dishes sail out of the kitchen; but regrettably it is as tasteless as the handsome waiters' service is impersonal. Even the red watermelon, bright orange honeydew and green grapes, which are so vibrant in color are lacking in taste.

At ten o'clock after the first toast, guests rise and proceed to the dance floor. It being too small for all who wish to dance tonight, they end up rubbing against each other to the sounds of the mercilessly loud music in the clouds of cigarette smoke. I am surprised to see Robik drinking heavily and sadly note that his once jet-black hair is now completely gray. He is surrounded by his family: his son Maxim, his girlfriend of six years, Tatyana; and his mother and a couple of relatives, none of whom I have met before. Maxim who is sitting on his left has grown from a cute chubby boy into a tall young man with a clean round face and broad shoulders. He yawns.

- "Where do you study, Maxim?" I ask.
- At Long Island University," he answers.
- "And what do you study?"
- "Physical therapy."

- "Do you like it?"
- "Nope." He answers honestly.
- "Then why do you study it?"
- "Well, I had to choose something," he shrugs his broad shoulders.

Both Robik's girlfriend Tatyana and his mother are sitting on his right. His mother's face has its usual stolid expression. She looks like a party member inspecting her troops at a Moscow Day parade. Hers is the only face that has undergone no change in the last decade. I think maliciously that after molding it God must have taken a look at his creation, dropped it like a hot potato and now it will never change. Tatyana has gained about thirty pounds since I last saw her. When did I see her last? It must have been five years ago at a New Year's party in their house. The union was still new. Christmas lights were on a palm tree near the window... dark red roses in a crystal vase...a roasted duck on the table. Guests were reciting poetry, playing the piano, dancing and telling stories.

By eleven o'clock all major sources of light in the hall of the restaurant go out and the dance floor is flooded with multi-colored stage lights. "Ladies and gentlemen! The performance is about to begin," the voice is booming out of the loudspeakers. "Please keep an eye on your lovely children." There are about seven kids wildly running around. A cute six-year old girl, all curls and frills keeps giggling and bouncing to the music like a rubber ball.

Dancers appear. In tall blue feathers with ornaments adorning their heads they look like a set of ponies. Their strong young bodies which have little space to move in and their pasted smiles make them look as if they've been taken out of the freezer and have not completely defrosted. The music is so loud that I am afraid my head may split like a coconut. A six-foot barely draped black giant, his pechtoral muscles glistening with oil like a well-polished leather shoe, bursts out from behind the scenes propelling a skimpily covered frizzy-haired blonde in his arms to stir our wildest fantasies. Each time he jumps I fear that he will land on somebody's head. When the performance finally ends I am greatly relieved.

My former admirer Sava, who is sitting across the table sees me wistfully looking at his golden watch and takes it for a sign of my interest in his expensive timepiece as well as his own persona. He takes the watch off his wrist and proudly presents it to me. After checking the time, I return it to him. It is ten to twelve. In ten minutes I can depart without hurting my host's feelings. Sava puts the watch by his plate. "Put it on or you will forget it." I urge him. "Forget it? Who? Me?" He lets out a loud tipsy laugh. "Don't worry, love. I won't forget it. This whole establishment can be purchased with this watch," he says proudly and casually runs his fingers through his dyed, carefully set hair.

Shortly after one o'clock I leave the party. A jobless Russian engineer who works as a taxi driver takes me home. Raindrops smear traffic lights all over the front window. He turns on a tape recorder and the sounds of old Soviet songs softly pour into the warm rainy night. He tells me that he's been living in this country for eight years and has just come out of a deep depression on account of his inability to find a job. He complains that wherever he applies for a position, they always ask him for references. He has none for he has never worked anywhere in the States besides the car service. I respond in the optimistic American fashion assuring him that everything will be all right. He listens to me and politely nods his head. He has heard it many times before.

When I come home the light in the corridor wakes Bruce up. He opens his eyes, mumbles something and falls back on his pillow. I lie beside him for a long time, pondering over the scenes, faces, smells and colors flashing through my exhausted tipsy mind and then fall into a troubled sleep. Next morning I wake up with a headache.

A BELATED BIRTHDAY

The old Presbyterian Church was located on Montgomery Street in Brooklyn, fifteen minutes away from the RR subway. We passed Trevor's house on the way there. I touched the heavy gate. Somebody must have just watered the flowers in the sandbox by his window, for the tiny drops of water were still trembling on their petals. I thought it peculiar that Trevor - who always had plans, tastes and dreams of such grandeur would plant those timid flowers, bright specks of color sprinkled over the happy greenery of the leaves.

The hollow silence of the cool chapel felt calming after the noisy heat of the street. A vase with a beautiful arrangement of exotic flowers and branches stood in a niche. About sixty people came, Trevor's brother, his sister-in-law, his niece and nephew among them. Nobody cried. I felt embarrassed and helpless, choking on a flood of tears. Time and again I tried to breathe the tears back in, but they just kept pouring out being controlled by some other will than mine.

Trevor's friend, a petite, carefully coiffured woman came to the microphone and read a speech. She finished it with the words: "Happy birthday, Trevor. You would have been thirty-eight years old last week." He was only thirty-seven. I carefully subtracted the numbers again. 1959 from 1996. Yes, he was thirty-seven years old. I always suspected that he was a little vain and didn't want to reveal his real age. Now I know that he wasn't.

Two black ladies got up and came up front, carefully balancing their big bodies on high-heeled shoes; they were precious goblets filled to the brim. One sang in German (pastor translated), the other in English. They sang about God, soul and eternity. I was listening to their strong sweet voices and asking, God, why Trevor? No answer came. I thought that the second tragedy of our times after losing God is that we lost all the answers. The white pastor got to the microphone and spoke about Trevor's sly smile and his love. He didn't elaborate, just said that we would always remember his love.

We left right after the service. I felt the cool spring breeze on my hot wet face. At that hour, there were less cars on the road. With traffic noise lightening, children's voices in the park became stronger and seemed to be closer. The late afternoon sun of the first hot spring day settled on the leaves, bushes and flowers. It was early June. Still untouched by the scorching heat of the summer, the first uncut grass stood tall, strong, glistening like rich fur of a healthy animal.

At six o'clock on a Friday afternoon people were coming home . From the back, many black men looked like Trevor, same T-shirt, same shorts, skinny legs in leather sandals, closely cut hair, slow gait of the people accustomed to moving their bodies in tropical heat. But among them there was no Trevor, nor there will ever be. Happy belated birthday, dear friend. Happy belated birthday.

*** Your Address Is No Longer In My Phone Book

_____
_____/////////// _____/////////// _____
/////////// _____/////////// _____/////////// _____///////////
// __

Your address is no longer in my phone book,
For you no longer have an address on this planet,
Nor social security number.
You're not concerned about your pension plan,
Your rent, your job,
You have no winter jacket.
And I still have one. . .
I mean the address, the pension plan, the job,
All that. . .
I also have an address book
With many names and telephones and faces,
Yours isn't one of them.
And on the page that your face used to live
Now sadness lives
And looks me in the eye
Each time I turn that page.
I miss you so,
But you
no longer
have an address
on this planet.

Irina with her friend, Trevor

THE LAST SURVIVOR

I see, young lady, that you've set your bicycle at level 3 speed. I'd like to know why you young people are always in such a rush. I've set my bike at level 0 and look, we are still biking side by side. It's not that I'm trying to teach you how to live, I just want you to know that you don't have to set your bike at a high speed. All of us here are doing the same thing and that's all that counts, right? Take me for example, I exercise every day. I come here early in the morning at eight o'clock and from here I go swimming.

- Where? In Coney Island?

- No, the water is too dirty there. I swim at Jones Beach. You know where Jones Beach is, don't you? Yes, it's right after Exit 23. It takes me about an hour and ten minutes to get there. I drive to the beach in the morning and I am back in Brooklyn at 3 o'clock. I work out every day, because once you stop, arthritis takes over. See these knots on my fingers? It's arthritis. So I've got to keep one step ahead of it, I've got to keep moving. And how often do you come here? I don't think I've seen you in the club before.

- Oh, I come here once in a while. I really don't have much spare time. I work in Manhattan, live in Brooklyn and have a hungry husband.

- Well, I've done my share. All that working and rushing, been there done that. Tell me, how old do you think I am?

- Oh, I don't know. I am very bad at telling people's age.

- Come on, give it a try.

- Well, maybe seventy. (thinking that he probably is in his mid seventies.)

- Aha! Wrong! I am eighty-four.

- Good for you! I would have never guessed.

- In my young years I worked very hard. During the depression I was a baker. My wife used to help me out at the bakery. We made a decent living. I came here from Czechoslovakia. She was of Czechoslovakian descent too, but she was born here. When I came to America, she was very young and we started dating right away. I had known her for seven years before we got married. We raised three boys together. She passed away three years ago, may she rest in peace. And where are you from? You look like you may be from Europe too.

- You're right, I am from Europe.

- Where in Europe may I ask?

- Latvia.

- Ah-a-a. that's near Poland? Lithuania is right next to it, isn't it? How long have you lived here? Eighteen years? You speak good English.

- Thank you. I studied languages at the University in Riga.

- Riga? It's the capital? You know last year I went back to Europe. My wife didn't want to travel to Europe. She was not interested. So we never went. What was Europe to her? She was born and raised here in the States. After she passed away I went to Europe by myself. I traveled all over: Poland, Hungary, Bulgaria and, of course, Czechoslovakia. Let me tell you, Europe has been destroyed. What the Germans had left, the Russians finished off. Most of the old buildings have been replaced by some ugly architecture. In my opinion, Stalin was worse for Europe than Hitler. The house I used to live in is still there though, but all the people who lived in it are long gone. I have a picture of a soccer team I used to play on. When I went to the local cemetery I saw that every one of those boys was lying there. I bought some nice flowers and put them on the graves. Then I went to the Catholic church in the center of Prague to say a prayer for them. There I spoke to the priest. I told him I was from America. He asked me if I had any family left and I told him that all my family had been killed. He asked me if I was Jewish and I told him, yes I was. "A Jew saying a prayer in a Catholic church?" he was surprised. "Look, Father," I said, "I am soon to meet my maker and nobody owns Him. There is a Jew on the crucifix right there. So here I am an old Jew from America saying a prayer for my soccer team in a Catholic church. All those boys were Catholic, you know." I gave him a donation too. Fifty dollars. There it's a lot of money.

226

Vow, look how quickly half an hour passes in a nice company. It's 12:30 already. Time for my swim. My name is Mike, and yours?
- Irina
- I enjoyed talking to you, Irina. Hope to see you around. Exercise is very important, you know. You've got to keep moving. Have a nice day. Bye."

Smiling In America

When Swami Rama, the founder of the Himalayan Institute in the Poconos first came to New York, he decided to take a stroll down Fifth Avenue, one of the busiest streets in Manhattan. He put on his best suit and went out. A young woman passing the hotel gave him a wide smile. And so did the other one who followed her. And the other one...Swami Rama thought that something was wrong with his outfit. He returned to his hotel and carefully examined his reflection in the big mirror. Everything was OK with his suit.

He went back to the street and when another young lady gave him a smile, he asked her why she was showing him her teeth. "You see in America we are taught to smile at other people,|" she said. "Even at those you don't know?" "That's right." He was very surprised.

Garbo once asked the reporter. "In America you are all so happy. Why are you all so happy all the time?? I am not always happy. Sometimes yes, sometimes no. When I am angry I *am very bad. I shut my door and I do not speak.*"

However, times are changing in America as well and yesterday I saw a young woman in Greenwich village wearing a T-shirt which said that women who pay their own rent don't have to be nice. And then the other one whose t-shirt said that she smiles only when she feels like it.

NEW SPEAK

Get on board to the now proper "Politically Correct" way of verbally expressing yourself. Don't say that someone is 'aggressive' but rather say 'assertive.' Nor should you say that someone is 'nosy'. Instead use 'inquisitive.' Please remember never say someone is 'fat' and definitely not 'obese.' Replace these with 'weight challenged'. 'Manic-depressive' is out , 'bi-polar' is in, so is 'crazy,' instead say 'eccentric.' No more 'give a round of applause,' it is 'give it up for.' A house wife is now 'a house engineer.' Finally remember there are no more 'problems' only 'issues.' And when that proper day of celebrating Mother's Day rolls around say, "May you all enjoy a Happy Female Parent Day."

The Closing

On a soggy Thursday morning in February Bruce and I were driving along the Belt Parkway on our way to Greenport. The compact Ford we rented for the trip tuned out to be quite temperamental. It kept on making squeaky warning sounds and neurotically was flashing suggestions on its screen:

"Check the cooler." "Trouble with the brakes," etc. Undaunted we proceeded through fog, wind, heavy rain and lightning. The car windows started fogging up and so I turned on the defroster which made the air warm and heavy and quickly put me to sleep.

I must have been out for over an hour for when I opened my eyes we were already pulling into the driveway of the house. Under the gray sky the house with its thousands of painted shingles loomed over us like a big wet white hen. I got out of the car and breathed in clean cold ocean air.

Misses Evans, the owner of the house arrived ten minutes later and let us in for a walk through. With all its furniture gone, the house had a forlorn depressed look about it. The paint was peeling off the walls, long cobwebs were hanging in the corners of the rooms. Looking at the curtain less windows one could see the imprint that thousands of rain drops had left on the dusty window glass over the years. What struck me most unpleasantly was the thick odor of mildew which is so characteristic of abandoned enclosed spaces in the country. The house seemed to be suspended in waiting, sad, apprehensive of its new owners. Misses Evans exhibited no emotion about leaving the place where she had spent fifteen years of her life. In her brisk businesslike manner she showed us where the thermostat was and warned us to set it at 60 degrees before we go away lest the pipes should get frozen.

We asked her who her neighbors were. "Two men have bought the house on the left," she said pointing to the big two-storied building with windows framed by old fashioned shutters. "they rent the second floor out and come here only in the summer on weekends. I haven't met the owners of the house on the right," she indicated looking at the small wooden cottage. "All I know is that they live in Sag Harbor and rent the house out to Section 8 people which is government subsidized housing, you know. I hardly ever see the tenants. The parents work in the daytime and their children are in a day care center.

The Italian family whose house you see in the back are very friendly. They have a small garden and in the summer they used to keep me supplied with tomatoes, lettuce and cucumbers so that I never had to buy them at the market. "Well, she said glancing at her watch , "I've got to get going. See you at the closing." With those words she handed us the keys to the house , got into her car and drove away leaving us to roam the empty dusty rooms, turn the faucets on and off, flush the toilets and try to figure out what each switch in the basement was for.

By the time we got back into the car and set off for Riverhead I had developed strong misgivings about purchasing the house. Why couldn't we continue renting the summer place in Sag Harbor which we had shared for years with an Irish couple that became our good friends? Why did we need this huge two-storied mildew-ridden responsibility? Was it too late to cancel this purchase? Did we have to go through with it even if we didn't feel like it? Couldn't we think about it a little longer? Before setting on the road to Riverhead we mad a U-turn in Greenport. A ship of mounting beauty was docked at the peer. She was standing there in all her magnificent proud splendor under the gray sky where the strong sea wind was angrily tearing thick heavy clouds apart. I took the sight of the ship as a good sign and decided not to voice my misgivings to Bruce who according to the silence that set between the two of us had plenty of his own.

Having arrived in Riverhead half an hour early we stayed in the car for a while trying to relax before the big event. Being too fidgety and restless we soon gave up trying, got out and headed for the green one-storied building where the business was to be conducted.

The heavy wooden front door opened into a spacious hall. Misses Evans was already there looking rather snug tucked in a tall plush armchair. Thick rugs, crystal chandeliers, white lillies in a crystal vase and an attentive soft spoken staff reminded me of a funeral parlor. I commented on this to Misses Evans. "It's quite impressive, isn't it,?" she agreed flashing her thick glasses at me. Our lawyer arrived ten minutes later and came over to introduce himself. So far we had talked to him on the phone only. He looked like a fat cheerful rabbit holding a big leather portfolio. As we shook hands I felt his soft warm palm. When Misses Evans' lawyer who had to drive in all the way from New Jersey had finally arrived, we all went into a spacious room and took our seats around a long mahogany table covered with glass, Misses Evans and her lawyer on one side and we with ours on the other. I found myself sitting opposite to Misses Evans' attorney, an attractive brunette of about forty, attired in a stylish black business dress. From her flushed face and shaking hand that held a sheet of paper I could tell that she was very nervous. Soon we were joined by a bank lawyer, a pink faced balding man in his mid thirties who was acting as a court jester, trying to relax everybody present by cracking jokes and being the first and often the only one to laugh at them. Two other ladies - the one from the bank and the secretary who kept walking in and out with a bunch of papers were both medium height, good looking blondes, tastefully attired , soft spoken with delicate white well manicured hands. They looked so much like two versions of the same woman that for a while I had difficulty telling them apart.

The bank lady brought in a big stack of copies and for the next two hours all four of them: the bank lady and the three lawyers engaged in exchanging the copies of the documents. I wondered how they managed not to get entangled in this endless stream of white sheets – who gets what and where it goes, but to my amazement everything proceeded quite smoothly, without any surprises or interruptions. In two hours I must have signed more papers than I had in my entire life including its remaining part. In the end I felt totally depleted of energy.

All that time Misses Evans sat quietly beside her attorney looking rather pleased like a kid under a Christmas tree suspended in happy anticipation. She had been trying to sell the house for two and a half years. Rolling her eyes in amazement at yet another sheet of paper that came her way she kept happily signing one document after another.

The door opened and Misses Evan's real estate agent, a short heavy woman in her late fifties entered the room triumphantly carrying her huge bust as if it were a tray on which an expensive antique cameo was displayed. I could almost hear the famous Verdi's march from Aida in the background to which the victorious troops are marching returning home. Proudly she landed next to the bank lawyer.

Suddenly his stomach growled loudly and hungrily. "Have you had any lunch yet," she asked leaning toward him. "No," he responded, "I make it a rule to have my lunch after the closing." "Here, " she offered him a box of tick-tacks, "This is all I have with me." "Are you implying anything?" he asked referring to the TV commercial about tick-tacks being a remedy for bad breath and laughed heartily at his own joke. Misses Evans' real estate agent smiled and comfortably established herself in a deep plush chair. She looked like a big cat spread on a warm radiator who after performing a series of tricks is relaxing in anticipation of a well earned reward. With everybody else in the room being so tense and businesslike her satisfied relaxed demeanor seemed almost inappropriate. Out of her pocketbook she produced two pictures of the house taken last summer from two different angles. Standing tall and white in the rays of the hot summer sun, surrounded by huge old trees, green bushes and bright flowers it looked much more attractive than what I remembered it to be on that particular cold and soggy morning. For a moment I stared at it in disbelief and then passed the pictures on to Bruce. After Bruce everybody else in the room took turns at examining them and politely expressing their approval of our new acquisition.

At last all the papers were signed and the house officially became ours, its sagging staircase, peeling paint, cobwebs, mildew, neighbors and all. Everybody sighed with relief and relaxed. After receiving her check Misses Evans' agent shook our hands welcoming us to the town of Greenport and the smiling bank lady presented us with a colorfully wrapped bottle of champaign after which Bruce and I went back to the house of our dreams fully determined to convert it from a dungeon into a palace.

Traveling Around

A Close Brush with Death

In November, 1984 Bruce and I decided to get married. Bruce was in charge of getting plane tickets and hotel reservations for our honeymoon. Our plane landed in Florida late at night.

Nonetheless, lurking in my mind I thought that it would be nice to take a dip in a lake near our hotel. Bruce was dead set against that. It was decided to do it early next morning. The next morning I put on my bathing suit and walked over to the lake. I became terrified when I saw submerged in the lake's blue water two pairs of alligator eyes looking at me with hunger. I then quickly ran back to my hotel room.

Swimming After The Storm In Puerto Rico

This happened in Puerto Rico off the Atlantic Ocean. Different people like doing different things in the summer. Some go berry picking, others like hiking. I like swimming. As long as I can and as far as I can. Wherever I go – I swim. In my country of origin, Latvia I was often prevented from swimming too far by our brave blue-eyed blond Latvian lifeguards. They would drag me out of the Baltic Sea as if I were a hungry kitten in a bowl of milk.

They would then threaten me with a fine. I was prevented from swimming too far, because of the danger. Peligroso (dangerous) would be written on signs everywhere on the beaches of Puerto Rico. The only place where there were no such signs was the Anne Wigmore

235

Institute in Aguada. There people were being educated about the benefits of a raw food diet. Chewing raw food and listening to the lectures left us little time for swimming. There being no lifeguards and no signs, I swam as far as I wanted whenever given a chance. Sometimes I could hardly see the Aguada Beach before I would turn back. That morning my friend Zelga from Sweden joined me for a swim. On the way to the beach we collected many colorful shells and baby coconuts that had been thrown down off the palm trees by a powerful storm the night before. When we came to the place where we usually swam we split. Zelga did not like to venture far into the ocean with its enormous turtles. I, on the other hand, jumped right in and swam so far that I could hardly see the beach. I saw a big palm branch in the water, one of those that angry storms break off and throw into the ocean. I swam to it and rested my head on it. The sun was hot the way it always is after a big storm and the ocean was calm. I had plastered myself over the branch and watched clouds overhead. They looked like lots of whipped cream. Then I heard a helicopter over me. There it was – a big noisy metal bird making circles over my head. After a while it flew away. Then on the left there appeared a boat with a big sign "Water Police" on it. Strange I thought as there is nobody as a rule in these waters at this time in the morning. There were some signs of a big storm from the day before such as baby coconuts and big branches of palm trees strewn all over. I decided that it was time to return to the shore.

When I came out of the water Zelga was nowhere to be seen. Instead, I saw the director of the Institute, Leola, hurrying toward me.

"Have they saved the man in the water?" she asked excitedly."

"What man? There was nobody but me."

- "No, there was a man clinging to a palm branch."

- "There was no man, it was me. I was not clinging, I was resting on the branch before swimming back."

- "No, it couldn't have been you, Irina. It was somebody in the middle of the ocean."

- "There was no one in the middle of the ocean but me."

So it was, the border patrol took me for a desperate Dominican Man who decided to enter the U.S. illegally through Puerto Rico and the Water Police was called. Well, was I proud of myself!

A Trip To Orient Point

Orient Point lies on the very tip of the North Fork on Long Island. We often take a bike ride to the Orient from Greenport. There we rest after a nine mile-ride, sip cold soda, watch the ships come and go and dream of all the places that we'd like to visit someday.

This Sunday we have arrived here later than usual. The hot sun is already high in the sky. The fall air is cool and smells of the sea and fish.

The ship at the dock is about to sail off to Connecticut. It's all white with red and navy blue stripes. She looks like a brand new-sneak floating on the blue ocean water. The sun is strong, so we settle down in the shade under the roof of a small outdoor eatery. We bite into big red juicy apples that we've bought at the stand on the way and watch a big lot full of cars and people empty into the ferry.

The parking lot between the pier and the ticket office is about two hundred yards long and a hundred and fifty yards wide. Now that it is finally free of cars and people, it becomes a huge empty space in which the melodrama of the late arrivals is played out as if on a giant TV screen.

First come two young lovers with their backpacks running towards the ship. They run in unison like a pair of trained circus horses, the sound of their boots echoing like hooves throughout the empty parking lot, the girl's ponytail jumping happily up and down.

They are followed by a pudgy middle-aged woman in a red dress, besieged by many packages that keep falling off her the way overripe fruit falls off a tree. She keeps bending down and picking them up.

As she is getting on the ship, a red headed woman in a gray pantsuit is running off it. "Timmy," she is shouting to the man in the middle of the parking lot who is walking towards the ship, "go back for the tickets! They don't sell the tickets on board, only in the ticket office!" The man takes a couple more steps towards the ship, then the information sinks in, he turns around and starts walking back towards the ticket office. "Hurry up!" the red-head is shouting, "they are about to sail off." The man starts trotting towards the ticket office. The last time he ran was thirty years ago. He's been sitting at the desk in his office without a window ever since. He struggles to pick up speed. Another fellow who is also running to get the tickets is closing up on him. He is much younger, in his late twenties, a stocky man with short legs, dressed in sneaks with a cigarette in his mouth. He is running so fast that his legs seem to be running ahead of him. "Don't run so hard," he shouts to the older fellow as he is passing him by, "you may get a fucking heart attack." In a couple of minutes we watch both of them run back to the ship, the young fellow's legs leading the way. As soon as they step on board, the ship lets out a long deep call and sails off.

That's when a gray Honda pulls up and three adults and a child get out. It is a young blonde with a child and her parents. They see the departing ship. "Why couldn't you get here a little earlier?" Her mother says to her. "Ma, we were both tired and I had to go to the bathroom," responds her daughter. She is on the heavy side, dressed in jeans and a windbreaker. The child is a little girl of about five years old. Her short light bushy hair ruffled by the ocean breeze makes her look like a dandelion in late spring that is getting ready to parachute its seeds out. Both women try to get over their disappointment at the sight of the ship sailing off and their annoyance with each other. They switch their attention to the child who wants to drink and depart in search of a store. While doing so they both keep talking to the child but not to each other. Throughout the whole scene the blonde's father, a tall gaunt man in jeans and a parker doesn't utter a word.

By now the ship is hardly seen. The apples have been eaten and the sun is going down. It's time to mount our bikes and ride back to Greenport. On the way there we'll stop in a Greek restaurant, order a jug of iced water, a warm pita bread and fried fish. Bye.

A Day In New Hope

We are having chocolate cream and cookie ice cream in an open cafe near the autumn stream in New Hope, Pennsylvania, and watching people parade on Main Street. The ice cream is slowly melting on my tongue leaving bits and pieces of roasted nuts, which I crush with my teeth. The little stream gurgles, talks and bubbles like a child having a conversation with himself. The fall air is crispy and goes well with the hot afternoon sun. I watch a family stroll over the wooden bridge – father, mother and son in his late twenties. The son's hand gropes for his camera. "Shall I take a picture?" He says looking at the stream. "Don't," his mother responds emphatically. "It's polluted." They leave.

Then three young people come. Actually they are not that young. I guess they are in their late thirties, but they feel and are dressed as if they were in their early twenties. All three look somewhat unripe to me.

The two men are dressed with great care. One of them, his reddish hair neatly cut and blown dry, is wearing shorts and a light beige cotton sports jacket. The other one, a younger man with dyed blond hair is wrapped in a dark woolen coat. A small golden earring is sparkling in his left ear. The woman is all denim. I notice a trace of mascara on her eyelashes as she takes her sunglasses off. Her brownish hair is going gray. She has a hungry unkempt look about her.

It seems they have just met. She is in the process of extracting a dollar bill out of her purse and giving it to the earring guy. She wants coffee. The redhead does the same. For some reason the earring guy is uncomfortable, his face is flushed. He takes the money and goes to get coffee. The redhead and the denim woman are looking for an empty table. All tables being occupied, they settle themselves on the steps of the ice cream parlor and talk about somebody they haven't seen for a while, i.e., he hasn't seen but she has, and now she is filling him in. While talking, she aggressively slices the cool fall air with her hand. Her hand's wrinkled, dry, bluish skin reveals the woman's age. They look too animated for this kind of information exchange. The earring guy reappears in the door of the parlor. "How do you want your coffee?" The man wants it regular, the woman wants it with a sweetener. When the earring guy returns with the cups of coffee, he is even more uncomfortable than before, for he doesn't know how to join their conversation, which is about somebody he doesn't know and neither of his friends knows how to end it.

The denim woman makes a sudden dash for an empty table. To save time she doesn't straighten up. Half-bent, paper cup in hand, she looks like a predator after its prey. She moves with a supersonic speed, the sound of her voice trailing way behind her. It all happens while one man is listening and the other one is painfully trying to enter the conversation. They both seem to be dumbfounded and somewhat relieved by her sudden disappearance, but they follow her voice and there she is, sitting at the table and motioning for them to join her and share her prey. Oh, the sweet smell of success. She did it. Nobody saw it, but she did. While everybody was enjoying themselves, she was working, she was watching she was searching for the table. Now she can relax.

"Oh, here comes Jill with her lovely smile," announces the denim woman. Enter Jill, a considerably younger creature, looking slightly dirty, but only to the point of not really being so. Jill who must be in her early twenties has a vacant stare of a woman who has been off dope for a while. She smiles wryly, imitating a biological response to her friend's saying that she's got a lovely smile and at the same time assuring everybody present that coming across such a lovely company as this one is an everyday occurrence for her.

The denim woman is smiling a satisfied smile of a Roman conqueror. She's got what she came here for. She's got her table, a cup of coffee with an artificial sweetener and two specimens of not so opposite sex sitting next to her. Now she is proudly displaying all these treasures to Jill. Her mission for the day has been accomplished. Tomorrow she will have something to tell her colleagues in the office about her weekend.

We finish our ice cream. It's getting close to four o'clock. The sun is going down. It's getting cold. We leave.

Summer's End

This is my last Thursday in Long Island. I am sitting in a little Greenport deli by the water where one can get a two egg sandwich, a cup of lukewarm coffee and a small carton of orange juice all for $1.50. Through the window I can see my red bicycle chained to a tree. I biked here eight miles from Sag Harbor and now it feels so good to sit on a chair instead of a hard bike seat. In the morning a Senior Citizen's Club congregates at the deli. They usually occupy two corner tables and have a loud and lively discussion centered around church. Today they are outdone by a group of boisterous teenagers who have come here for breakfast. School has started, which reminds me that next week I'm going back to the city, to its overcrowded subways, exhaust fumes and tired people. Red, yellow and brown leaves will slowly circle all the way to the ground, filling the air with their rich fermented smell. If the weather stays dry these leaves will make a crunchy sound under my feet. In the fall birds get to be very very restless and noisy in the morning. They occupy the top branches of the tall old trees and scream and shout like a big family that is packing and getting ready to leave. Soon they will spread in long triangles across the sky. I remember the sadness with which my mother used to watch birds leave Latvia in August. Their departure would signify the beginning of eight long cold and rainy months.

I leave the deli and stroll along the shore listening to the gentle talk of the waves. Seagulls perched on the buoys and walking on the sand look like beach vendors waiting for customers.

Back in Sag Harbor, Main Street looks like an empty hall after a party and the guests have gone home. The sea breeze is rolling strips of paper, empty soda cans and plastic straws on the ground where just a few days ago happy crowds were strolling on their long suntanned legs, dressed in shorts and summer dresses walking their mistresses and dogs, wives and children, husbands and lovers, licking dripping scones of home-made ice cream from a corner store.

Even though the greenery is still strong and abundant, many other colors are gone. Gone are the happy flowers from the flower beds. Gone are the bright dresses of girls and young women. Local folks either don't pay much attention to the way they dress, or else dress very conservatively. Gone are the wide brimmed straw summer hats, fuschia-colored balloons from the entrance of the flower shop on Main Street. And so are the white, yellow and orange sail boats that looked like a bunch of butterflies that descended into the blue waters of the bay. Gone is the long line of impatient bikers from the front of the bike shop, anxious to get back on the road. The crowds have departed and so have their fancy cars, sailboats, bikes, kites, dogs, colorful beach umbrellas, parasols and incredible bathing suits that leave nothing to one's imagination.

I'm writing this sitting on a bench near the water.

Goodbye till next spring, sunny island.

Silence

I have often asked those who live in the country: "Well, it's lovely here in the summer. But what about in the winter when it is cold and windy and everything is covered with snow?"

Today I woke up in the mountains, at a place which is three and a half hours drive from the city. It's a glorious morning. My window is like a framed picture. The world is buried in deep fluffy snow. The naked black branches of the tall strong birches are frozen in the pale morning air. I am watching snowflakes first playfully chase each other, then give way to thick falling snow falling from the sky. Sometimes I get lost in the movement as it seems to me that instead of falling the snow seems to be rising. Just to make sure I move closer to the window and look out. The only reminder of civilization is an old green, red and yellow van which out of my window looks like a toy abandoned by a child whose mother's voice sent him scurrying home. Soon it too will be covered with snow.

How strange it is to observe this constant movement that produces no sound. In the city where I live every movement is accompanied by noise. This movement that is initiated by heaven, this silent dance of whiteness hypnotizes me. My limbs grow pleasantly heavy. The picture in the window of my room draws me to it. It makes me think of purity, virginity, death. . . If I knew how to pray I would.

The Seasons of New York

In the golden, green and red world of Christmas parties,there is plenty of food, drink and dance.

In the streets people are carrying colorful boxes and packages.

The world that denies us the main things in life, creates so many other needs.

We wrap them up and give them to each other.

The cold has frozen all the smells, and my guts are no longer turning over, as I pass the homeless sleeping on the pavement, their feet sticking out of huge cardboard boxes.

In the windows smiling mannequins seductively display bridal gowns and veils to the world of dead marriages.

A pale bald man is banging desperately on a phone trying to get his quarter out; cold wind is blowing snow flakes on the naked torsos of men and tender skin of women in jean ads.

They make me shiver.

Spring is so far away.

Before spring comes, it sends a moan of passion into the air. In New York Spring doesn't come, one day it just happens. On the first spring day people's faces look creased like a hat that had spent the whole winter stashed in an overstuffed closet. When at night, overworked and overdressed I drag my tired feet back home, winter clothes weigh heavily on my exhausted frame. I feel intoxicated as if I had just emptied in one gulp a bottle of magic potion that was supposed to be taken by a spoonful, and now it has simply knocked me out. It was supposed to change my perception and make things wonderful and mysterious, but now I am drunk and all I want to do is to get into bed and sleep it off. The next morning it is too late to celebrate for it's already summer. It's hot, the garbage on the corner stinks and the gray polluted city air is squeezing its merciless paw on my throat.

Oh, to find myself in Greenwich Village in New York on a summer day that isn't hot, but just right is like a blessing from heaven. From my bench I see a little farmer's market that has sprung on the corner of a cobble stone street. Like a horn of plenty, the buckets on the tables are overflowing with green zucchini, yellow string beans, red tomatoes and purple eggplants. The sea of flowers, lilies, roses and marigolds covers another table. A lovely young woman in a long yellow silk skirt is choosing a bouquet of roses. A smiling young farmer is helping her, taking flowers out of the bucket, showing them to her, enjoying the beauty of a woman whose attention is engrossed by the flowers. Her lover, a young woman in jeans and a red T-shirt is watching the scene from afar resentfully and sullenly.

My Signature Hat

I got this hat on our trip to Canada. It was exhibited on a mannequin in the window of an expensive boutique located on the main avenue in Montreal. I paid $90 for it. It was a woolen beret that was sliced like a bialy that was ready to go into a toaster. Then a strip of dyed fur was sewn in reconnecting both slices and upgrading the beret to a hat. The hat was a hazel color which is the color of my eyes. Somebody has invented this hat and there is no human head that fits into it better than mine, may I humbly say. When I was younger I looked in it like a lady in a carriage in the famous portrait painted by the famous artist, Ivan Kramskoi. It carried me back all the way into the eighteenth century. I have been wearing it for the last twenty years and I've been often complimented on it on the streets of New York. "I like your hat," people say to me and I thank them.

Once a year I lose this precious hat and go through a familiar cycle of first going to the lost and found department at work where a security lady asks me in horror, "Oh dear, you've lost your signature hat? Again?" And I sadly nod my head. Then I go home and turn every closet upside down. I also search for it on our coat tree in the corner of the veranda, and I even call the last eatery I went to for dinner to see if I have left it there. "No! No hat!" Heartbroken, I finally accept the fact that my hat is no longer a part of my reality and tearfully say my goodbyes to it, only to find it the next day curled up like a cat in the back seat of my car or patiently hanging on a hook under my jacket. I grab it, I kiss it, and fondle its silky fur. I tell it how much I appreciate it and I could swear I can hear it purr.

About a decade ago as I was walking on the street in Manhattan, I raised my eyes and saw Mike Wallace admiring my hat.

- "Honey, I said to it, you are being appreciated."
- "I know, it grumbled, somebody should.
- "I love you."
- "I love you too."

To the hand that has sewn my hat and to the heart that has come up with its design I bow my head and say thank you.

Irina's Signature Hat

A Cat Lady

I am wearing a dead woman's pants. In her late years she lived alone in a two-storeyed house with her four cats. She spent a lot of time lying in her bed surrounded by them watching a shopping channel while the cats were watching her. The images on the screen agitated her mind until she called the number on the screen and ordered the item demonstrated to her by tall slim girls.

After her death her daughter brought the four cats to the animal shelter and took the clothes her mother had ordered on the shopping channel to the opportunity shop. This is how the second hand store in our town is called. I found them there, many still with price tags and wonder if she had ever tried them on. I bought three pairs of pants: red, black, and blue. That's how they ended up on me. I bike in them.

Incidently, the proceeds from the opportunity shop support the animal shelter where her cats went to live. So the balance in the universe has been properly maintained. I'm wearing a dead woman's pants.

This excerpt was taken from the Russian Magazine, "I Love," (June 26, 2007) based on an interview with Irina Martkovich when she visited Latvia.

Cinderella Visa Versa by Olga Zubareva

Like Cinderella, Irina found her happiness thanks to the unique size of her foot. Only the fairy-tale heroine's foot was miniature whereas Irina's was size forty-two. In the 1970's Soviet industry manufactured shoes for women only up to size forty-one medium. That's why Cinderella visa versa often had to be satisfied by wearing men's footwear. In the end she got so tired of this that she immigrated to America. This summer Irina Martkovich visited Latvia for the first time and told us the following which was published in the Latvian Magazine "I Love!" by Olga Zubareva. In

Search of the Right Shoe when her friends did not think that this reason was valid enough, I said, "Try to walk just in one shoe one size smaller than the other one, then you will understand me." For some reason, nobody has agreed to participate in this experiment.

But, if we want to be serious the end of the 1970's was very difficult and when there was a possibility to leave Latvia I decided to follow my suitcase. I could go to Canada or Australia, but one of my students and his family – I used to teach him English in Riga – decided to go to New York, and I joined them. Soviet people often try to stay together.

My first impression of Brooklyn, where we were placed in a home for senior citizens, was quite unpleasant. There were piles of garbage everywhere. After an orderly Riga it was difficult to get used to seeing such an unsanitary sight in Brooklyn where we were assigned. In Manhattan we were overwhelmed by the wealth and energy of the area which was never seen by me before – the subway is very ugly, but quite convenient, - so you get used to it. As far as the stores are concerned, my Riga colleague saw in a deli five different sorts of mushrooms which made her burst into tears, saying, "Americans will never understand us."

Of course I was in a better situation than other immigrants, because having learned English since the age of five I knew it very well. When I started working as a secretary in an American school, I was asked to substitute for a sick teacher. By the end of the class the students asked me to take her place permanently. The school administration where I was working as a secretary gave me other classes which I taught for twenty years. First, I taught immigrants from the Soviet Union and then ESL students from all over the world. I also made the following discovery: Women learn languages quicker than men. We like to communicate using gestures, facial expressions, while even those men who know the language well remain quite shy for some time. While the level of education helps people to learn a foreign language; Americans readily accept everybody, because they themselves at some point are the descendants of immigrants. I was also very lucky because my colleagues were very educated people.

I first met my husband, Bruce, at a supermarket where I asked him to get me a jar from the top shelf which I was unable to reach. That's how we got acquainted and then got married. We came into the City Hall in New York which reminded me of a combination of a railway station and a public rest room. There were long lines of people applying for marriage certificates. We had to fill out a long application. After doing so we signed it and asked an officer there if we had done everything correctly. "Yes, you have she answered." We stayed in the same apartment where we had spent thirteen years. After this I decided to change my place of employment. With my new job which was then more lucrative than Bruce's employment, I applied for health insurance. There in the personnel department I was asked to provide a marriage license which I did. A couple of days later I was informed by the personnel department that what I showed them was not a marriage license, but rather a marriage application. That's why we had to return to City Hall and obtain a marriage license, amid a few smiling faces there who worked in that department. We were told that this department had mailed us thirteen years before the proper form to fill out with a date to appear to officially be married in court, however, due to the fact that we had then just moved to another apartment we never received these necessary papers.

To the age of forty Bruce worked as a social worker. After that he requalified as a wonderful massage therapist, trying his new skills on me. In the meantime, I was discovering yoga for myself. In Latvia every summer I was spending my time in the country. Summers in New York can be brutally hot and one of those summers I spent at a yoga retreat in the Poconos. This is how I became interested in yoga and involved my husband in it too. Since then neither of us have experienced back pain and are considerably flexible and rarely get sick. Otherwise, we have a whole generation of young people who are not able to bend or exercise regularly when they are willing to let go of their smart phones.

247

For many years we used to travel to Puerto Rico. There at the Ann Wigmore Institute we listened to the lectures about the benefits of eating a raw food diet. Unfortunately we cannot become fully raw. We have learned to make different unheated cakes. Local food is so wonderful it's a shame to heat it. I also used to swim a lot in Puerto Rico. Once when I came out of the water I saw the "Water Police" and later learned that they were looking for a man who earlier was holding onto a palm branch in the ocean. That man was me. The "Water Police" was under the impression that he was trying to get into the U.S. From the Dominican Republic. Aquarius is my sign and I'm destined to love water to a great extent where I immerse myself in it for long periods of time.

At first, mother land would not forget me. I took part in the conference named "Russians Are Here." There a Russian English teacher from the Soviet Union approached me and started interviewing me in Russian as to where I am from, asking if my relatives were still living in the Soviet Union and where they lived. For some reason I felt uncomfortable answering her questions until I realized that no teachers from the U.S.S.R. were allowed to travel abroad. She was a KGB agent which was confirmed by two FBI agents whose visit shortly followed hers. Obviously they were following each other throughout the conference. Soon after that some KGB agents came to my parents' apartment and ransacked it. What they were looking for remains unknown for they found nothing.

We travelled around the world a lot. I especially was fascinated by our trip to England. The problem was that since my college years I have been visited by a schizophrenic camera thought of there being no such thing as an England in the world. We were told that in order that we would continue to work more for little money and to keep us in fear of other countries. When I was waiting for my husband in one of the halls of Madam Tussaud, a man covered by camera equipment came up to me and examined me looking for a sign of my name. Having found none he realized his mistake when I moved. He dropped his camera and asked for my forgiveness and ran away.

My remembrance of Latvia is full of the deep friendships that I had there. After emigrating I lost touch with many of these precious people because I did not want to put them into any danger where the Soviet authorities would see that they had contact with an emigre. Now that we are free, let 's travel and see each other more often.

A NEW PROFESSION

After trying several professions, Leonid, a marine engineer in the Soviet Union, has become a vacuum cleaner salesman in the U.S. He sells vacuum cleaners walking from door to door. He also calls people on the phone, having picked out Russian sounding names from the phone directory. Once he comes upon the name of Maria Pavlova, and sees that she lives close by. He dials her number. A soft woman's voice answers the phone and invites him over. Leonid arrives at her door with his vacuum cleaner. Maria, a plain short woman with thick ankles in her early thirties opens the door and offers him a bowl of borscht. He accepts her invitation.

They sit down at the table and talk about New York, high food prices, how difficult it is to find a good apartment in a decent neighborhood. He is recently divorced. She came to the States alone. By the end of their conversation she says, "Okay, let me help you out." She takes a big brown bag into which goes a stainless steel pot, a meat grinder, a colander and they go to Leonid's apartment. On the way there they go to a Key Supermarket where they buy a chicken, some vegetables, potatoes, carrots, and a head of cabbage. When they get to Leonid's place she makes him a hearty soup and stays in his apartment. A couple of weeks later as they are sitting on the sofa in his living room watching television, Leonid says to her, "Maria, you are a nice gal. Let me be honest with you. I went through a nasty divorce. I'll never marry again, but I have a good friend, Yury Petrenko, who is dying to get married. Would you like to meet him?" She sighs, says, "Okay" and gets her big brown bag into which she puts her stainless steel pot, meat grinder, and colander. Leonid drives her to his friend, Yury. After a month Yury finds himself a rich bride in Queens and asks Maria to move out. Maria leaves.

Half a year passes by. In Spring New York explodes into yellow colors of Forsythia bushes, as beautiful tulips bloom on every corner in Manhattan. Young children are brought to playgrounds. Things start looking better for Leonid. He has become one of the leading vacuum cleaner salesmen of his company. He has bought himself a Chevrolet and a leather jacket. The car is not new, but it looks good. One day as he is driving in Brighton, he sees Maria walking down the street carrying her big brown bag and looking tired and forlorn. He opens the window. "Hey, beautiful," he shouts out to her. "Would you like to have a ride?" She stops, looks at the man in the car and recognizes him. All of a sudden she emits a loud scream and starts banging on the hood of his car with her big brown bag. The bag falls apart and the stainless steel pot, the meat grinder, and the colander roll out of it onto the ground.

EPILOGUE

Each time my teacher Anita Nachischione comes to New York from Latvia, she asks me the same question. "Irina, have you ever regretted your decision to leave Latvia?" To which I always say, "Never." Not even for a moment, even during the most trying times did I regret the decision I had made thirty years ago to leave my country. There are things that I miss terribly. I miss strong relationships people develop in Latvia, the cleanliness of Riga streets, the beauty of its architecture, Latvian refined taste in arts and its educated populace. I miss little cafes in old Riga, its theaters and concerts. But no matter how beautiful the surroundings and relationships may be for me freedom is the air without which I cannot survive. In 1991 Latvia became free, but it will take many more years for the scars to heal. The art of freedom has to be learned. Many regard freedom as being a right, but very few regard it as being a responsibility.

Seeing other peoples and their cultures has enriched me tremendously. I have finally satisfied my hunger for adventure and come to view each new country as a variation of my own self. I have also come to understand that allowing everything is as destructive as forbidding everything. I see society as a garden that has to be cultivated. You don't fertilize the weeds along with flowers and vegetables or they will eventually overcome the garden and suffocate all the flowers. Finding the balance between freedom and restriction is a delicate thing that requires a wise gardener.

There are certain ills that befall this part of the world as well, but between the ills of the new world and those of the old one, I choose the former.

In the end let me tell you another joke.

Abram Abramovich keeps emigrating from the Soviet Union and coming back. Finally he is summoned into the KGB headquarters where he is placed in an empty room, handed a globe and ordered to stay there until he has finally chosen the country that he will not come back from. After a couple of hours he emerges from the room. When a KGB man asks him if he had chosen the country, he sighs and asks, "Comrade Ivanov, do you have another globe?

CPSIA information can be obtained
at www.ICGtesting.com
Printed in the USA
BVHW051024230723
667676BV00003B/48

9 798885 273572